UTTAR PRADESH
Etawah
BHIND
GWALIOR
DATIA
Orchha
Hamirpur
Banda
Mahoba
Ken Gharial
Kalinjar
Khajuraho
Chitrakoot
Jaunpur
Allahabad
Bhita
Ranipur
Dhubela
CHHATARPUR
Ajaygarh
PANNA
Rajgarh
Madla
TIKAMGARH
Lalitpur
SATNA
REWA
SIDHI
Dubri
Maihar
VINDHYA RANGE
SONE
Panpatha
SANJAY (DUBRI)
GOVIND BALLABH PANT SAGAR
Bagdara
SAGAR
DAMOH
Damoh Plateau
KATNI
Tala
UMARIA
BANDHAVGARH
SHAHDOL
Baikunthpur
BHANRER RANGE
Singorgarh
Noradehi
JABALPUR
FOSSIL PARK
NARMADA
NARSIMHAPUR
DINDORI
Premnarayan
Amarkantak
MADHYA PRADESH
Pachmarhi
MANDLA
Phen
Achanakmar
Korba
Bilaspur
KANHA
Kawardha
Janjgir
CHHINDWARA
SEONI
Kukrai Plateau
BALAGHAT
PENCH
Khawasa
CHHATTISGARH
Gondia
Ramtek
Nagzera
Nagpur
Bor
WAINGANGA
MAHARASHTRA
Tadoba
Garhchiroli
Chandrapur
Adilabad
Manikgarh
Kawal
Pranhita
NH 2
NH 92
NH 91
NH 25
NH 86
NH 96
NH 76
NH 27
NH 7
NH 75
NH 26
NH 78
NH 12
NH 12A
NH 69
NH 6
NH 200
AFGHANISTAN
PAKISTAN
CHINA (TIBET)
DELHI
NEPAL
BHUTAN
INDIA
BANGLADESH
MYANMAR
BHOPAL
KOLKATA
MADHYA PRADESH
MUMBAI
HYDERABAD
ARABIAN SEA
BAY OF BENGAL
BANGALORE
CHENNAI
Lakshadweep
Andaman & Nicobar Islands
SRI LANKA
INDIAN OCEAN
N

AN EICHER GOODEARTH PUBLICATION

Copyright © 2008 Eicher Goodearth Pvt. Ltd., New Delhi
ISBN **978-81-87780-73-1**

Editor and Publisher: Swati Mitra

Design: Ritu Topa
Editorial Team: Anupriya Roy, Bodhisattva Sen Roy, Nidhi Dhingra
Photographs:
Ananda Banerjee pp 70-71, 78-79, 85B, 86A, 95B, 96A;
Ashok Dilwali pp 58B, 59M; **Joydip Kundu** p 67A;
Mallar Sarkar pp 62-65, 66B, 67B, 69A&B, 73-75, 76B, 77B, 95A, 96B;
Micheal Vickers pp 78A, 81B, 83A; **N C Dhingra** pp 80-81, 82B;
Nidhi Dhingra pp 4-10, 12, 13B, 14A, 15-23, 25-27, 28A&B, 29B,
30-34, 35A&B, 36-50, 51B, 52-53, 54AR, 56-57, 85-86, 88-94;
Krishna Kumar p 68B;
Swati Mitra pp 13A, 14B, 60-61;
Tarique Sani pp 66A, 72B, 76A, 77A
Cover Photograph: Nidhi Dhingra

The photographs on the following pages have been reproduced
with the kind permission of INTACH: 24M, 28M, 29M, 35M, 51A, 54B

Text Contributions: Sharbani Chattoraj (Land and History pp 4-12);
Adheer Somvanshi (Box on Yogini Cult p 52)
Endpaper Map: Advisor - Lt. Gen (Retd.) S M Chadha
Illustrations: Nidhi Dhingra pp 71B, 72A, 76A, 84-85

Special thanks to:
Ashwani Lohani, Managing Director, MP Tourism
G S Chahal, Executive Director, MP Tourism

All rights reserved. No part of this publication may be reproduced, stored
in a retrieval system, or transmitted in any form or by any means, electronic,
mechanical, photocopying, recording or otherwise,
without the prior permission of the copyright owner.

Great care has been taken in the compilation, updation and validation
of information, and every effort has been made to ensure that all information
is as up-to-date as possible at the time of going to press.
Details like telephone and fax numbers, opening hours and
travel information may change.

However, the Publishers are not responsible for errors, if any, and their consequences.
The Publishers would be happy to receive suggestions and corrections
for inclusion in the next edition.

Please write to Executive Publisher, Eicher Goodearth Pvt. Ltd.,
Eicher House, 12 Commercial Complex, Greater Kailash II (Masjid Moth),
New Delhi 110 048.
Email: goodearthbooks@eicher.in

This publication has been supported by
Madhya Pradesh Tourism

Printed by Aegean Offset Printers, New Delhi
on behalf of Eicher Goodearth Ltd.

CONTENTS

Land and History — 4
Narmada — 13

Exploring Jabalpur — 16
Madan Mohan Fort — 18
Balancing Rock — 22
Rani Durgavati Museum — 23
Cantonment — 26
Old City — 30
Pisanhari-ki-Madhiya — 36
Bajnamath — 38
Tilwara Ghat — 39
Tripur Sundari Temple — 40
Bhedaghat — 42
Marble Rocks — 44
Dhuandhar Falls — 48
Chausath Yogini Temple — 50

Excursions from Jabalpur — 55
Bargi Dam — 56
National Park of Fossils — 58
Mandla Fort — 58
Pachmarhi — 59
Amarkantak — 60
Wildlife Parks — 62
Bandhavgarh — 64
Kanha — 70
Pench — 74

Education — 86

Phrase Book (English-Hindi) — 87

Practical Information — 88

LAND AND HISTORY

'Lofty and spreading *mahua* trees stud the plain; and its surface is scoured by the numerous and rapid streams which, pouring down from the Satpura Hills during the rainy season, have cut for themselves a passage to the Narbada [Narmada] through the soft soil' *(Imperial Gazetteer,* Vol 10). The city of Jabalpur is located in this picturesque Narmada valley, lying at the junction of the Vindhya and Satpura ranges.

The stunning Marble Rocks at Bhedaghat

JABALPUR

The most prevalent theory regarding the origin of the name 'Jabalpur' is that the city is named after sage Jabali, who is believed to have meditated on the banks of the Narmada. Others have variously derived the name from:

> the Arabic word *jabal* (granite boulders), referring to the rocky landscape;
>
> *Jauli Pattala* (a sub-divisional unit), mentioned in Kalachuri inscriptions;
>
> Jauli, the Huna princess, queen of the Kalachuri king Karna.

The British name for Jabalpur was a variation only in terms of spelling: they spelt it 'Jubbulpore'. However, even this minor deviation became a bone of contention in 1937 between the Commissioner of Jubbulpore, Mr. Greenfield, and the Deputy Commissioner, Mr. Grigson. The latter considered the ten letters in the word 'Jubbulpore' inordinately time-consuming and preferred 'Jabalpur'; while the Commissioner, prompted by more practical considerations such as the use of the name in stamps and railway tickets, thought the change utterly inadvisable. Eventually, the two came to a unique compromise: each was free to use the spelling he preferred and the other would recognise it! (M. C. Choubey in *Jabalpur: The Past Revisited*)

Above: *A palash tree in full bloom*
Below: *A view of Jabalpur from the top of Madan Mahal Fort. The landscape around Jabalpur is characterised by huge boulders* (jabals) *which give the city its name*

'The valley of the Narbada from Jubbulpore to the western boundary is an alluvial flat, chiefly composed of a stiff red or brown clay with numerous intercalated bands of sand and gravel.

Imperial Gazetteer, Vol 14

The Deccan Trap near Jabalpur is the richest dinosaur field in India. The first dinosaur fossil was found by Captain William Sleeman, better-known for his role in the suppression of thugees *(see box on p 11)* in Jabalpur cantonment, as early as 1828. There is, in fact, a species of small dinosaur named the *Jubbulpuria tenuis*, described by Charles Matley and Friedrich von Huene in 1933. This 1-2 m long carnivore lived in the Upper Cretaceous period, 70 million years ago.

JABALPUR

In ancient times, the settlement here was known as Tripuri (modern Tewar, 12 kms from Jabalpur). Legend has it that Tripuri was the capital of three *asuras* – Tarakasura, Maya and Vidunmali, who were defeated by Shiva. There are numerous references to Tripuri in the *Mahabharata* and the *Puranas*. In the ancient times, it was an important town, lying on the routes that connected Kaushambi, Vidisha, Mahishamati and Ujjayini. The site was first discovered by Lt Col Yule of the Bengal Engineers in 1860-61.

Top and Right: *2nd century Satvahana inscription from Baghora, Jabalpur; 11th century sculpture of Shiva's head (both at Rani Durgavati Museum)* Below and Bottom: *sketch of the Chausath Yogini Temple, Bhedaghat; Sri Varahi, one of the yoginis at the temple*

Tripuri was part of the Chedi kingdom (one of the 16 Mahajanapadas) in 6th century BC. Then it came under Mauryan rule, as is shown by the discovery of an Ashokan rock edict at Rupnath (82 kms from Jabalpur), dated to 272 BC. The fall of the Mauryan empire in 2nd century BC resulted in the formation of the republican city-state of Tripuri.
In 1st century BC, it was captured by the Satavahanas. Their reign was followed by the rule of the local dynasties of the Bodhis and the Senas, who were finally uprooted by Parivrajaka Maharajas, feudatories of the Guptas in 4th century AD.

In 7th century AD, the Haihaya Kalachuri kingdom was founded by Vamaraja, with its capital at Tripuri. The greatest king of this dynasty was Lakshmikarna. In 1055, at the height of his powers, he controlled all of central India. He even declared himself *chakravartin*. The Jain poet Kanakamara wrote: 'When the Kalachuri king [Lakshmikarna] moves his brigade in war, the primordial tortoise starts moving. Because of the movement of the turtle, the earth also moves, so much so that the mountain Sumeru also trembles. The heavenly Gods become unsteady. This is the result of Karna's movement in war.'

However, the Kalachuri kingdom began to decline soon afterwards, and in 13th century, it was conquered by the Gonds. The founder

Land and History

of the Gond dynasty who ruled over the Garha-Mandala kingdom, with Jabalpur as its capital, was Yadava Rai.

The greatest Gond ruler was Sangram Shah (1510-1543). He conquered 54 *garhs*, comprising modern Sagar, Damoh, Bhopal, Mandla, Seoni and the valley of the Narmada. He is also credited with building the Chauragarh and Singorgarh Forts, and Sangram Sagar Lake in Jabalpur.

Sangram Shah was succeeded by his son Dalpati Deo, who ruled rather uneventfully till his death in 1550. As Dalpati Deo's son Vir Narayan was only five years old, his widow Rani Durgavati ascended the throne. The legendary Rani ruled for 14 years, unifying Gondwana under her banner.

Like other Gond rulers, Durgavati also built tanks to store water; one can still see the Ranital built by her. A devotee of saint Vallabhacharya, she patronised the Radhavallabh Sampradaya. She is said to have invited Vallabhacharya's son, Vithal Nath, to her capital and given him a gift of 108 villages.

She repelled the attack by the Malwa Sultan Baz Bahadur in 1556. However, this hard-earned peace was not to last long. In 1564, Mughal emperor Akbar's army, led by Asaf Khan, marched to Gondwana. Even though Rani Durgavati's 5,000-strong force was no match for the ten times larger and better-equipped Mughal army, she refused to surrender and instead met her adversary in battle at Narrai. Her forces repelled the enemy thrice, but eventually, the weight of greater numbers and better artillery proved to be decisive. Refusing to suffer the dishonour of defeat, Rani Durgavati stabbed herself to death.

Above: A painting showing the seige of the Singorgarh Fort
Below: Statue of Rani Durgavati mounted at her memorial site, on the Jabalpur-Mandla road

JABALPUR

For the next 25 years, this region remained under the control of Akbar. In 1591, it was returned to the Gonds, on the condition of acceptance of Mughal suzerainty. Gond control came to an end in 1781, when the Marathas took over and added the region to the Peshwa's Saugor territories. In 1796, Jabalpur and surrounding areas came under the exclusive control of the Bhonsles of Nagpur.

In 1817, after the Battle of Sitabaldi, British forces took possession of the town and made it the commission headquarters of the Narmada territories. The Jabalpur cantonment was set up in 1826 over an area of 445 acres.

> The first Boy Scout troops in India were started at Jabalpur, Bangalore and Kirkee in 1909. Two years later, the Girl Guide movement began in Jabalpur.

> An interesting, though inadvertent result of the British presence in Jabalpur was the invention of snooker. Colonel Sir Neville Chamberlain, while relaxing at the officer's mess, suggested that a number of coloured balls be added to the usual pyramid pool variation of billiards. The word 'snooker' is said to be a concurrent invention. When a young subaltern tried his luck at the new game and missed a shot, Chamberlain remarked that he was a 'regular snooker'.

In 1857, Jabalpur was garrisoned by the 52nd Native Infantry. However, when the deposed Raja of Garha-Mandala and his son, charged with conspiracy against the British, were blown away from cannons; the entire regiment quietly left the station.

The L-60 Anti-Aircraft Gun sits handsomely at the Shaheed Smarak Chowk in the Cantonment area

In the old times, the dense forests of central India posed many perils, both natural and man-made. This region was notorious for a secret cult known as Thugee, whose members committed ritual murder to express their devotion to goddess Kali, or Bhawani. The newspaper *Samachar Darpan* reported in 1833 that 100 thugs on an average murder 800 people in a month!!!

The legend regarding the origins of Thugee talks about a demon called Rakatbijdana who started devouring men at the beginning of the world, without even a drop of blood spilling on the ground. Goddess Kali decided to stop him and wiping the sweat from her arm, produced from it two men. She gave them a handkerchief to put all demons to death; hence the signature weapon of a thug was a scarf with which he would strangle his unsuspecting victims.

The man responsible for freeing central India of this horror was a British officer named Colonel William Sleeman, appointed superintendent of the Thugee and Dacoity Department in 1835. Relying heavily on information given by captured thugs, he succeeded in hanging 400 thugs and imprisoning many more. A plaque in his honour was installed in the Christ Church Cathedral by his nephew J. Sleeman, and a town has been named after him called 'Sleemanabad'.

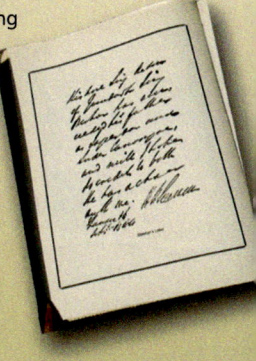

In 1861, the Saugor and Nerbudda Territories (which included Jabalpur) became part of Central Provinces, which in 1903 was renamed as Central Provinces and Berar.

Jabalpur was witness to several important landmarks during the national movement, such as the meeting of the first Provincial Conference (1906), the institution of a branch of Home Rule League (1916), the establishment of Mahakoshal Provincial Committee (1920), the Flag Satyagraha (1923), breaking of the Salt Law (1930) and the Quit India movement (1942-1944).

A very significant event here was the Tripuri session of the Indian National Congress (1939), held at Tilwara Ghat on the banks of the Narmada.

The Tripuri Congress session is significant as it witnessed a rift between Mahatma Gandhi and Subash Chandra Bose, when the latter defeated Gandhi's nominee in the elections

JABALPUR

After independence, Jabalpur was assimilated into the state of Madhya Bharat, and later into Madhya Pradesh. Today it is the headquarters of the district with the same name. It is a major educational hub and an industrial centre. The several defence manufacturing units here, include the Gun Carriage Factory, Vehicle Factory and Grey Iron Foundry.

Jabalpur Through the Ages

3rd century BC	Part of the Maurya kingdom
1st century	Republic city-state of Tripuri is established, and later captured by the Satvahanas
7th century AD	Part of Haihaya kingdom
13th century	Gond kingdom is established
1510-1543	Reign of Sangram Shah, the greatest Gond king
1550-1564	Reign of Rani Durgavati
1564	Battle of Narrai between Rani Durgavati and Mughal forces led by Asaf Khan
1789	The region comes under Maratha control
1798	The territory is given by the Peshwa to Bhonsles of Nagpur
1817	Battle of Sitabaldi; British capture the region
1857	52nd Native Infantry leaves their station
1923	The Flag Satyagraha
1939	Tripuri session of the Indian National Congress
1947	India becomes independent; Jabalpur becomes part of the state of Madhya Bharat
1956	Jabalpur is included in the newly-created state of Madhya Pradesh

NARMADA

'I fell in love with the Narmada the moment I saw her. She was incontrovertibly feminine, more so than any other river I have seen. A dazzling blue, gentle and beckoning... it seemed to offer a lasting relationship based on warmth and affection.'

– *Bill Aitken*, Seven Sacred Rivers

The main west-flowing river of the subcontinent, Narmada rises at Amarkantak, over 3,000 feet (914 m) above sea level, and meanders through 1,250 kms of beautiful broad-leaved forests and fertile plains before joining the Arabian Sea off the coast of Gujarat. Barely six feet (1.8 m) wide at its inception, it eventually discharges a volume of water equivalent to the combined flow of the Ravi, Beas and Sutlej, into the sea.

Above: *River Narmada, at its inception at Amarkantak, is a thin stream*
Below: *At Bhedaghat, the river falls with a thundering force forming the spectacular Dhuandhar Falls*

JABALPUR

Flanked by the Vindhyas in the north and the Satpuras in the south, the river makes a natural barrier between north and south India. For much of her course she is like a mountain stream, roaring over falls, leaping over rapids, rushing through canyons, occasionally pausing languorously in deep pools, and hence is often referred to as Rewa or the 'leaping one'.

But she is also Mananada, who brings bliss, Rajini, the spirited one, Kamanda, who fulfils desire, and Vibhatsa, the terrifying.

Narmada is one of the seven sacred rivers of India – the *saptaganga*. It is said that while the Saraswati makes holy Kurukshetra, the Ganga makes holy Haridwar, Prayag and Kasi, the Narmada makes sacred whatever she touches.

A charming folk tale speaks of Ganga, dressed like a dark woman, visiting Narmada to take a purifying dip in its waters!

There are numerous legends regarding the creation of Narmada. A popular one holds that she was born of the sweat from Lord Shiva as he performed his *tandav nritya* (dance of destruction). Therefore another name for Narmada is Shankari – the daughter of Shankara.

Another legend goes that, once, on the peak of Amarkantak, Shiva sat in a trance for a long time. The very beauty of his calm poise, the magnificence of that total immobility, suddenly took a form, that of a sweet damsel. He blessed her saying, 'you've inspired tenderness *(narma)* in my heart, you are Narmada' and granted that she always remain free. However, smitten by her beauty the *devas* pursued her, and as one tried to get hold of her, she turned into a river and slipped through his fingers, flowing as the holy Narmada.

One of the most arduous Hindu pilgrimages involves performing the Narmada *parikrama* or circumambulation of the entire length of the river. A centuries-old ritual, it starts in the beginning of *kartik* (October-November), and takes three years and 313 days to complete.

Above: *A sadhu drinking water from the holy Narmada*
Left: *Narmada Udgam Temple at Amarkantak*

Devotees spend their days walking along the river bank and sleep in temples along the way. In today's times however, many pilgrims take a bus or a jeep.

Like the Narmada, the Son also originates at Amarkantak; however it flows eastwards in the opposite direction. An endearing legend tells the story of these two rivers: 'The Son was betrothed to Miss Nerbudda and was proceeding with a *barat* (wedding procession) to fetch his bride; she was curious to see what he was like and sent little Miss Johila (a small stream joining Son) to spy. Son met this young lady and fell in love with her; so Miss Nerbudda got in a furious temper, threw rocks about and, with a terrific kick, sent them bounding over the precipice towards the east, while she proceeded in the opposite direction.' – *Faiths, Fairs & Festivals of India* by Major C.H. Buck.

Running westwards, the Narmada flows through Jabalpur, where spumes of foam rise in a fine mist from the Dhuandhar Falls, as it spills over a thirty foot (9.14 m) ledge. The river then slides into a deep pool and passes through the famous two-mile long marble gorge. On an occasion even the towering white marble cliffs were unable to contain the river in flood.

Lovingly called Narmada *Mai*, she is worshipped annually on the occasion of Narmada Jayanti, when thousands of oil lamps are floated from the sprawling Sethani Ghat of Hoshangabad.

On her onward journey, Narmada's next major destinations are Omkareshwar, the island shaped like Om, and the Holkar capital of Maheshwar. Thereafter, skirting the northern border of Maharashtra she flows through Gujarat before emptying into the Arabian Sea near Bharuch.

> Ma Rewa, tharo paani nirmal,
> Chal chal behto jaye re
> Amarkant se nikli Ma Rewa
> Jan-jan karti tharo sewa
> Sewa se sato pawe mewa
> Ved-Puran bataye re
>
> — Lyrics of
> *Ma Rewa*, Indian Ocean band

Above: Near Jabalpur, the Narmada flows through the magnificent Marble Rocks gorge

JABALPUR CITY MAP

- Hanuman Tal
- OLD CITY
- Kamania Gate
- Bada Phuvvara
- Victoria Hospital
- Clock Tower
- Ambedkar Chowk
- Madhotal
- High Court
- Jyoti Cinema
- Russel Chowk
- Railway Station
- Rani Durgavati Museum
- Kalchuri Residency
- Veterinary College
- to Airport
- to Tripuri and Bhedaghat
- Sadar Bazaar
- CANTONMENT AREA
- to Mandla

Sketch map not to scale

EXPLORING JABALPUR

Madan Mahal Fort
Rani Durgavati Museum
Cantonment
Old City
Pisanhari ki Madhiya
Bajnamath
Tilwara Ghat
Tripur Sundari Temple
Marble Rocks
Dhuandhar Falls
Chausath Yogini Temple

The city of Jabalpur stands in a rocky basin surrounded by low hills, about 9.6 kms from the Narmada river. Dotted with *ghats*, broad roads, and a relaxed pace of life, it is a welcoming relief from the rush of the metros. The gorge of the Narmada at Bhedaghat, where the river passes through the well-known Marble Rocks, is about 22 kms away.

MADAN MAHAL FORT

Madan Mahal Fort is situated to the southwest of the modern city of Jabalpur, close to the Balancing Rock. As recorded in the *Imperial Gazetteer*, Vol 14, 'Garha [was] once the capital of the Gond dynasty of Garha-Mandla, whose ancient keep known as Madan Mahal, still crowns a low granite range with the old town lying beneath it.' It is 'a small building of no architectural pretensions', and is yet striking, for its structure is quite unlike any other – the fort being perched on the top of a hill on a huge boulder of rock! This peculiar construction and its picturesque setting have earned for it much admiration and marvel.

> 'High on the cliffs overhead, a huge boulder preserves a delicate balance on a base some four inches square. The precarious poise of this rock could be taken as the symbol of Jabalpur' –
> Dom Moraes,
> *Answered by Flutes*

JABALPUR

The fort is reached by a long flight of steps, cutting through the rocky landscape strewn with trees, hedges and boulders. A three-storey structure, it has multiple balconies on each floor. The main arched entrance looks on to the narrow winding staircase, which leads to the upper floors. Dominating the skyline, the fort commands magnificent views of Jabalpur town and the valley around.

Remnants of smaller structures in the complex can be seen in the ruins of archways and low walls edged with cupolas. The rooms in front of the fort, with arched entrances, probably lodged the troops of the rulers who stayed here.

Tradition and folklore attribute the fort to the Gond ruler, Madan Shah, who supposedly built it in 1116. The fort is believed to have served as his pleasure palace. Some scholars surmise that the fort dates back to Rani Durgavati's reign when it was used as a watch-tower owing to its strategic position.

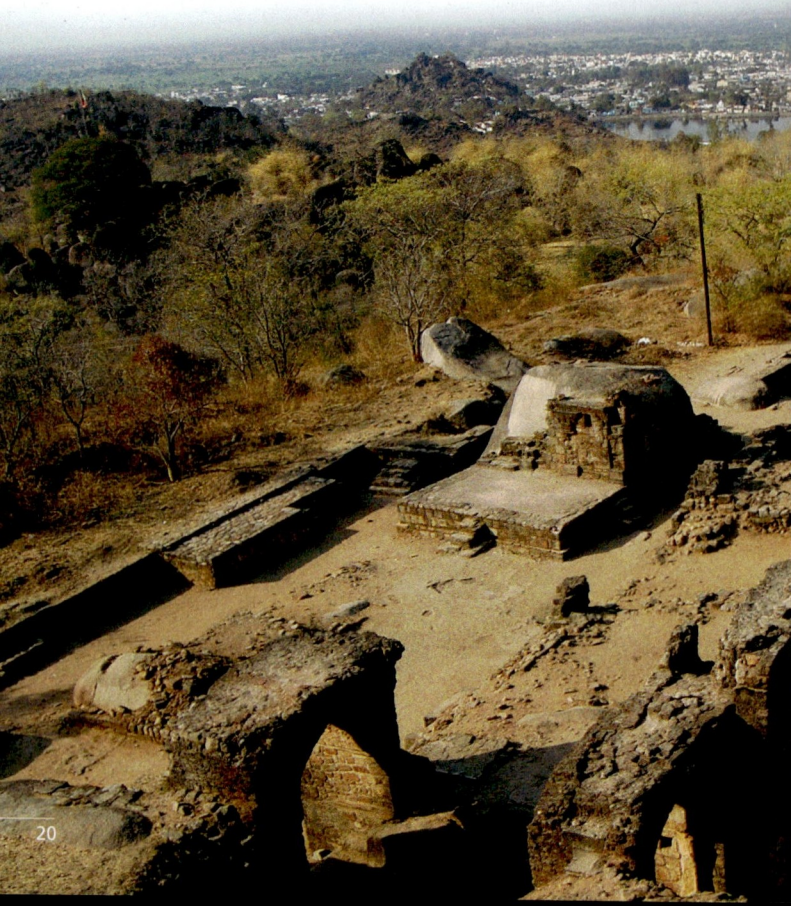

Above: *Steps leading up to the fort*
Below: *View of the fort complex from the top*

However, the stone slab outside the fort, among other things, claims that it was built by the Gond ruler, Hridayshah, when he shifted his capital to Ramnagar, Mandla. 'In the sixteenth century the capital [of the Gonds] was removed to Mandla, and importance of Garha declined.' (*Imperial Gazetteer*)

The maintenance and protection of this historical monument has now been undertaken by the Archaeological Survey of India (Bhopal Circle).

Halfway up the steps to Madan Mahal fort is a Shiva temple, Sindh Pancheshwar Bholenath Mandir.

Above: *Columns on the upper floor*

Close by is the **Balancing Rock**, which never ceases to fascinate viewers. Perhaps a result of eroded volcanic rock formation, it has a huge rock balanced on another with just human finger-thick nexus. It is said that this precarious balance has even withstood earthquakes.

RANI DURGAVATI MUSEUM

Timings:
10 am - 5 pm
Mondays closed
Entry fee: Rs 10

Dedicated to the memory of the great Gond queen, Rani Durgavati, is the museum named after her, situated to the south of the Sadar Bazaar.

In 1964, on the occasion of Durgavati's 400th martyrdom day, a proposal was set forth for setting up a museum in the city. Thereafter, on 24th June, the then Chief Minister, Pt. Dwarka Prasad Mishra laid down the foundation in Pt. Motilal Nehru Park.

The museum houses nearly 2,900 architectural remains, including a fine collection of sculptures, inscriptions and prehistoric relics. The largest collection is that of art objects dating to the Kalachuri period.

Above: *13th century Parmara inscription from Hoshangabad*
Left: *Prastara inscription*

The galleries on the ground floor display 10th-13th century stone sculptures of deities of various religions – Hindu, Jain, Buddhist – found from excavations in and around Jabalpur. There are images of Shiva, Ganesh, Bhairava, Buddha and the Bodhisattvas, Parsvanath and other Jain *tirthankaras*, among others. The intricately carved figures of Uma-Maheshwar are the most numerous as well as the most fascinating.

Above: *This 10th century sculpture depicts Uma-Maheshwar as engaged in playful dalliance*
Left: *Elaborately carved sculpture of Jain tirthankaras, dating back to the 10th century*

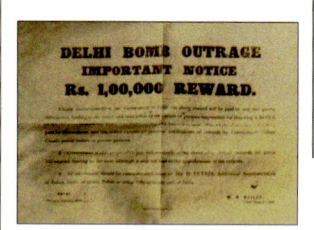

JABALPUR

Above: *Exhibits in the gallery dedicated to India's Freedom Struggle*

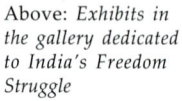

A separate section in the museum is dedicated to the nationalist leaders, as Jabalpur was deeply involved in India's freedom struggle, and was oft-visited by the nationalists. The gallery has exhibits of letters and photographs; particularly those of Mahatma Gandhi, Jawaharlal Nehru and Bhagat Singh.

Above left: *Image of a yogini from the Chausath Yogini Temple*
Above right: *Photograph of the temple complex*
Below: *11th century Varah sculpture from the Tewar region*

Interestingly, the 10th century Chausath Yogini Temple at Bhedaghat has an entire gallery to itself, with pictures of the temple complex and of the 81 *yogini* sculptures installed in the niches of the circular wall around the temple.

Also worth visiting are the tribal section, and the coins and inscriptions section on the upper floor.

The tribal gallery is done up very handsomely with bamboo and thatch. Hut-shaped panels on the wall showcase the various tribal exhibits, and endearing miniature models depict the tribals engaged in various activities.

Mandla, near Jabalpur, is a significant tribal belt in central India. Gonds and Baigas form the most numerous of the tribal groups here.

Top: *A view of the tribal gallery*
Above: *Domestic scene in a tribal hut*
Left: *Baiga bride and bridegroom dressed elaborately, wearing traditional jewellery and headgear*
Below: *Free standing sculptures on display in the museum compound*

With their unique culture, traditions and way of life, the tribals form an integral part of our rich heritage. A dominant characteristic of tribals of this region is the art of tattooing and their love for jewellery.

CANTONMENT AREA

> 'Jabalpur is a pleasant city…It is quiet and spacious, and in what is still called the cantonment area the houses possess a certain splendour. Bougainvillea and hibiscus adorn the hedge: trees shade the avenues. Outside the city the Narmada makes a broad, blue, rippled streak between high, wrinkled cliffs of pure white marble.' – Dom Moraes, *Answered by Flutes*

When the British subdued the Marathas in 1817, among the *jagirdars* who still controlled important villages around Jabalpur was Krishna Rao Paswan, who owned the entire land which is now called the Cantonment. The British took possession of this area by paying him a meagre compensation. Set up in 1826, the Cantonment had an area of 445 acres kept aside for it. With the arrival of a second regiment in 1837 the area was enlarged; and by 1861 the total area was 524 acres. (*Jabalpur: The Past Revisited* by M.C. Choubey)

Open and clean with broad roads, the Cantonment area clearly stands out from the

Interesting sculptures don the roundabouts throughout the city

rest of the city. Apart from the residential quarters of the officers and the troops, and the training institutes, it also has the Military Hospital, Government grass farm and a military dairy.

> 'Jubbulpore is well laid out, with broad and regular streets, and numerous tanks and gardens have been constructed in its environs. The climate is comparatively cool, and Jabalpur is generally considered the most desirable of the plain stations in the Central Provinces' – *Imperial Gazetteer*, Vol 14

Interestingly, nearly all roundabouts in the Cantonment area are marked with an impressive sculpture installed in the centre. A majority of them are statues of important nationalist leaders, such as Dr. Rajendra Prasad and Dr. Bhimrao Ambedkar, whereas others are intriguing sculptures such as the globe with three figures atop it, at the Srijan Chowk. The Shaheed Smarak Chowk has the L-60 Anti-Aircraft Gun sitting handsomely in the middle.

The 40 mm L-60 Gun was manufactured at the Royal Ordinance Factory in 1904. Its first use was by the British during the Second World War. After Independence, the gun was used in the war against China in 1962, and thereafter was used repeatedly until it was given to the Central Ordinance Department for safe-keep in 1983. It was later donated to the Jabalpur Cantonment Board as a war trophy, and on 15 August 2003 was installed there, at the Shaheed Smarak Chowk.

The Cantonment also has many magnificent colonial structures, such as the Law Courts, Commissioner's Residency and Empire Theatre.

Commissioner's Residency

Built in 1821, the Commissioner's Residency is one of the oldest official residential houses in India that is still in use. The British built it soon after they took over the city from the Marathas, and it served as the residence of William Sleeman. It has high circular pillars and a portico. The Residency was the focal point during the Uprising of 1857. Approached through the Commissioner's office and the garden, the building cannot be seen from the main road.

The Law Courts

The High Court complex, completed in 1889, remains one of the most beautiful and imposing edifices in Jabalpur. Designed by Henry Irwin, the building is characterised by Gothic arched openings and brick columns. It originally housed the

Collectorate, the District Court and the Treasury. With the formation of Madhya Pradesh in 1956, when Jabalpur was chosen as the seat of the state's High Court, this building became the court building, with the collector's office moving to a new location nearby.

Narmada Club
Built in 1889, the Narmada Club stands within landscaped gardens. Formally registered in 1904, its main feature is the centrally located dancing hall.

Empire Theatre
Nostalgia rewinds as one visits Empire Theatre, situated in the heart of Civil Lines. The building façade is circular in plan with a balcony on the first floor. In the past, drama troupes from as far as Britain performed here on the semi-circular platform. Initially, it served as a stage for classical plays, including Shakespearean productions; however, with the coming of cinema, silent movies and subsequently talking movies came to share the platform here. It was the best place to watch English movies. During the 1950s, Prem Nath, the famous Bollywood actor, bought the theatre from Bellamy, who ran a ballet dancing school. Unfortunately, today it stands in a crumbling state.

Churches
The English Methodist Church (1874-83) and the Christian Bible Church (1906) built at Civil Lines, are the two most important churches of the city.

OLD CITY

Years ago, the Omti Nala formed a sort of unofficial dividing line between the Civil Lines and the Cantonment on one side, and the main town and *basti* on the other. In stark contrast to the appeal and fashion of Sadar Bazaar, was the densely populated hubbub of the town market. To western eyes, the shops built in narrow lanes appeared quaint and full of mystery. The area in the recent times has developed beyond recognition, yet the relative contrast between the old town and Sadar area continues.

A marked difference can be seen as one enters the old city area from the Cantonment. Much like the old part of most Indian states, the old city of Jabalpur is characterised by narrow, winding lanes bustling with people, local transport and stalls laid outside the shops.

The main bazaars here are the **Omti Bazaar**, with the clock-tower and the **Omti ki Masjid** as significant landmarks, the **Badaa Phuvvara Bazaar** close to **Kamania Gate**, and the **Gorukhpur Bazaar**. The busiest bazaar intersection near Lordgunj, Bada Phuvvara is named after the famous *phuvvara* or fountain built by Raja Gokuldas in 1883, to commemorate the completion of the Khandari Water Works project.

The busy Omti Nala intersection, with the Omti ki Masjid standing tall

Kamania, the gateway to this area, is itself a relic of the pre-British period, when Jabalpur was a Maratha *suba* under the Bhonsles of Nagpur. Kamania comes from *kaman*, meaning a 'bow' or 'arch', which forms the lower part of the gateway. The clock which adorns the gate was added in 1939 to commemorate the historic Tripuri Congress Session held nearby, at what is now called, the Tilwara Ghat *(See p 39)*.

The Gond rulers had a penchant for tanks and step-wells – a large number of them being excavated for irrigation, and to serve as reservoirs in times of drought. Ranital, Cheritcal, Adhartal, Thakurtal are amongst the many that were constructed during Rani Durgavati's reign. It is said that there were 52 tanks in all in Jabalpur.

Today, however, majority of the tanks have dried up, or have been built over and large colonies have sprung up in those areas. Adhartal, named after Rani Durgavati's minister, Adhar Singh Kayastha, is now the site for the Agriculture University. Ranital, named after Rani Durgavati, is where the new Sports Complex is being built, and the Marhatal, has become the present day commercial hub of the city.

Kamania Gate continues to be the most significant landmark of the old city area in Jabalpur

While you are in town, a must-try is the local specialty – the *khoya jalebi*. Though the *khoya jalebi* can be had in some other parts of the country as well, Jabalpur boasts of its most delicious and true preparation.

A good place to try *khoya jalebi* would be the popular sweet shop, Badkul Mishthan at Bada Phuvvara.

The 17th century Devtal is one of the cleanest water bodies of Jabalpur. Referred to as Vishnutal in Gond chronicles, it has stone embankments, *ghats*, *chattris* and temples all around. It is held that Acharya Vithalnath, son of saint Vallabhacharya, stayed very close to Devtal.

The most historic and significant *tal* is **Hanumantal**. It was excavated in the late 18th and early 19th century, most probably by the Gonds. It was later fortified by the Marathas, and developed upon by the British. It is recorded to have covered an area of 21 acres at one time. Today its area is 17 acres or 6800 sq m. (*Hanumantal: A Case Study in Revitalization of Inner City Areas* ed. by Meera Dass and Ishwar Dass). It also has the most water, and unlike the other *tals*, has the appearance of a lake.

Hanumantal is the core of the inner city area. Here the streets are narrow and lanes narrower still, and they house the *kothis* of the rich and the powerful, interspersed with temples, both large and small. Twenty-five temples and shrines stand in the immediate vicinity of Hanumantal, of which 15 are in the inner ring, facing the tank.

The two *havelis* or mansions worth looking at here are those of Anwar Mehboob and Raja Gokuldas. **Anwar Mehboob's** *haveli* has receding terraces creating a pyramidal profile. Close by is the multi-storied *haveli* of **Raja Gokuldas**, which was constructed in the first decade of the 19th century. It is an opulent building, with breathtakingly-intricate stonework.

A white marble complex of the **Digambar Jain Temple**, visually dominates the scene. Seventeen domes, each with a *garbhagriha* within, loom large, forming a distinctive skyline. The temple has magnificent interiors with extensive glasswork and marble flooring.

One of the bigger temples here is the **Bari Khermai Temple**. Many temples of Vallabh Sampraday dating back to the 17th century also stand around Hanumantal.

Of the mosques in the area, the most significant is the early 20th century **Mohammadi Masjid.**

In 1868-69, Hanumantal was in a very bad condition, and a donation was made by Raja Gokuldas for its refurbishment. Today it presents a mixed canvas comprising the Jain Temple, and other smaller shrines; bustle of industrial activity like textile dyeing, godowns; children playing, people gambling, fish market; an auto-rickshaw stand and the police station.

Architecturally, Hanumantal area has a unique character that is difficult to recapture in modern development. The uniqueness of the place is constituted by its visual scape, historic character, ritual landscape, and cultural character.

Marble domes of the Digambar Jain Temple dominate the visual scape at Hanumantal

JABALPUR

Among the most prominent colonial structures in the old city is the **Victoria Hospital**, now known as **Seth Govind Das Hospital**. When it was built in 1876 it was one of the most beautiful hospital buildings in the country, with comfortable accommodation and all facilities for both European and Indian patients. The Victoria Hospital doubled as the Jabalpur Medical College Hospital from 1955-68, till the Medical College was shifted to the Tripuri Campus.

Presently known as **Gandhi Bhawan**, the **Victoria Town Hall** was inaugurated on 2nd September 1892, to commemorate the Jubilee year of Queen Victoria's reign. Standing next to Victoria Hospital, it has a rectangular structure with an imposing porch and a statue of Gandhi in the front. Apart from a well-stocked library, the Gandhi Bhawan also accommodates the University study centre and a reading cell.

Above: *Victoria Town Hall with the sprawling lawns in front*
Below: *The clock-tower stands on a roundabout in the old city*

In 1881, a suitable site was selected at Khandari to construct a reservoir, the purpose of which, as highlighted by the then Chief Commissioner, Sir J. H. Morris, was to provide 'an abundant and unfailing supply of sweet and pure water.' The **Khandari Water Works** was the pride of the Central Province, and has lived up to its purpose through the years. Today, however, the city draws only a part of its water requirement from this reservoir.

In olden days, whosoever came to Jabalpur would certainly pay a visit to **Govind Bhavan** and could not remain untouched

Old City

In 1867, the East Indian Railways flagged off the Naini (Allahabad)-Jabalpur Block rail traffic. Since then Jabalpur has been firmly placed on the main railway line from Kolkata to Mumbai.
A narrow gauge branch line connecting Jabalpur with Nagpur was constructed by the Bengal-Nagpur Railways in 1905.

by its breathtaking opulence. This *kothi* was constructed in 1909 as the residence of Rani Chunni Bai, Raja Gokuldas' wife. It was elegantly furnished with the best German and Dutch furniture and a crystal fountain in the formal sitting room.
Years later, when the family fell into debt due to their wholehearted participation in the Gandhian movement, this magnificent palace was mortgaged and subsequently handed over to creditors. It now lies forlorn; a major part of the building being occupied by the government R.T.O office.

Standing close to the railway station is the **Raja Gokuldas Dharmshala**. The imposing building was built by the Municipal Committee in memory of Raja Gokuldas, and was opened to the public in 1911.

Above: *Photograph of the Govind Bhavan as it looked in 1992*
Below: *Gokuldas Dharmshala with (right) a statue of Raja Gokuldas at the entrance*

RAJA GOKULDAS
1839-1908

JABALPUR

PISANHARI KI MADHIYA

Eight kms from the railway station, on the Jabalpur-Nagpur road is a cluster of Jain temples, known as Pisanhari ki Madhiya. It has 13 *jainalayas* or Jain temples standing atop a 91.5 m high hill, amidst scenic pathways of carefully laid-out plants and flowers.

Built in stone, these temples are believed to be nearly 650 years old. Legend has it that the temples got their name from a simple woman who started them with money earned from milling flour, saving it penny by penny. They are thus seen as a symbol of her dedication and service.

The largest temple however is constructed at the foothill. Covered with a vaulted roof, it has a *mandapa* and a double-storied *garbhagriha*. The interiors of the temple display marvellous artwork, with sculptures of 152 Jain *tirthankaras*, carved in marble, seated in small shrines.

Pisanhari ki Madhiya

Built over an area of 18 acres, the temple complex also includes a *gurukul*, a *brahmi vidyashram*, an administrative training centre and an ayurvedic medical hall. The *dharamshala* (resthouse) has both regular rooms as well as luxury rooms.

Various views of the Jain temple, Pisanhari ki Madhiya. Stunning marblework characterises the temple interiors.

Situated at a distance of about 20 kms from the city, is the **Pariyat tank**, where a dam has been built at the source of the Pariyat river. A major source of water, it is also a popular picnic spot.

Eight kms from the city, the **Sea World** water park, is a new attraction. Equipped with slides, pools, raindance floor and a café, it is an ideal place for spending a hot summer day. Swimming costumes are available here on rent.

Another place for leisure sports and activities for the youngsters is the **Jabalpur Sports Club**, situated on the Jabalpur-Mandla road. The complex boasts of a bowling alley, swimming pool, discotheque, and also offers facilities for arranging parties.

JABALPUR

BAJNAMATH

Situated about 15 kms from Jabalpur, Bajnamath temple was built by the Gond king, Sangram Shah between 1480 and 1540.

A narrow lane bustling with activity, with stalls selling red cloth, *prasad,* and other *puja* paraphernalia on both sides, leads to the temple. It is variously dedicated to Bhairav and Shani.

Reached by a long flight of steps, the temple is a square structure, facing east. The open courtyard in the middle is flanked by a raised platform, with the *garbhagriha* on the left and an open shrine of Hanuman on the right.

The bulbous dome over the *garbhagriha* is visible from afar. It is painted pink and yellow – colours popularly used in temples of central India. Called the *tantrik bhavan,* the *garbhagriha* is dedicated to Bhairava. Huge crowds of devotees throng the temple every Saturday, the day of Shani. Groups of men playing loudly on the *dhol* (drum) add to the mystique of the place.

The temple overlooks a man-made lake, **Sangram Sagar**, the openness of which makes for a surprise change from the courtyard bustling with activity.

> Shani, embodied in planet Saturn, is one of the *navagraha* or the nine celestial beings of Vedic astrology. Considered to be the strongest malefic and a stern teacher, he is often depicted as dark in colour, holding a sword, arrows and two daggers, and variously mounted on a black vulture or a raven.
> Shiva, Vishnu and Hanuman are also worshipped in Shani temples, believed to reduce his malefic effects.

TILWARA GHAT

Jabalpur is dotted with a number of *ghats* along the banks of the Narmada, which make for most of the scenic views that one encounters.

Close to the Tilwara bridge is Tilwara *ghat*, perhaps the most significant of the *ghats* in Jabalpur. It was from here that Mahatma Gandhi's ashes were immersed in the Narmada. An old Shiva (Tilwadeshwar) temple is located here.

Less than a kilometre from the *ghat* is the venue of the 52nd Congress Session, convened in Jabalpur in 1939. It was called the Tripuri Congress, named after the ancient town of Tripuri. 'Huge arrangements were made for the session… a new township was erected with all modern facilities for telephones, telegraph, bank and hospital.' (M.C.Choubey)

The Congress Session took place in a red dome-shaped structure standing on a square plinth, built atop a hillock. Even today the Indian National Flag is hoisted on the site.

The Tripuri session is significant in modern Indian history because of the rift that occurred between Mahatma Gandhi and Subhash Chandra Bose during the proceedings. Bose was re-elected president, defeating Gandhi's nominee, Dr. Pattabhi Sitaramayya. Soon after the election, however, several members of the Congress Working Committee resigned, and eventually Bose himself was forced to resign.

Below: *The venue of the Tripuri Congress*

TRIPUR SUNDARI TEMPLE

Situated about 12 kms from the city, in village Tewar, on Bhedaghat road, is the Tripur Sundari Temple. It is a significant Durga temple near Jabalpur, popular among tourists both from the city and outside.

On entering the temple, one is awed with the play of red and gold all around. Coconuts wrapped in red cloth are tied in every nook and cranny, presenting an intriguing sight. These are tied by devotees in the hope that their prayers will be answered.

The main image in the *garbhagriha* is of a three-headed goddess, representing Durga, Kali and Saraswati. An inscription at the entrance claims that the Kalachuri king, Lakshmikarna installed this image in the 7th century. The *prasad* from the temple includes a red and black bangle for female devotees.

Daily, around noon, the otherwise serene atmosphere of the temple suddenly reverberates with the rhythmic drumming of *dhols* and the sound of the *shankh* blowing, to announce the time of *bhog* (when *prasad* is offered to the goddess). The temple complex also includes a *yagya shala*, where *yagyas* (sacrificial fire) are performed.

The temple is particularly crowded during *navratri* festival, celebrated here with great fervour during the month of April.

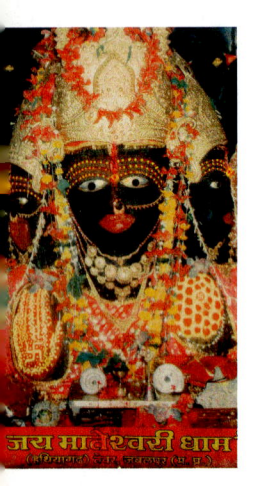

Above: *Poster of the main idol in the* garbhagriha
Below: *Stalls outside the temple selling* prasad *and coconuts*
Facing Page: *Temple interiors with coconuts wrapped in red cloth tied throughout*

41

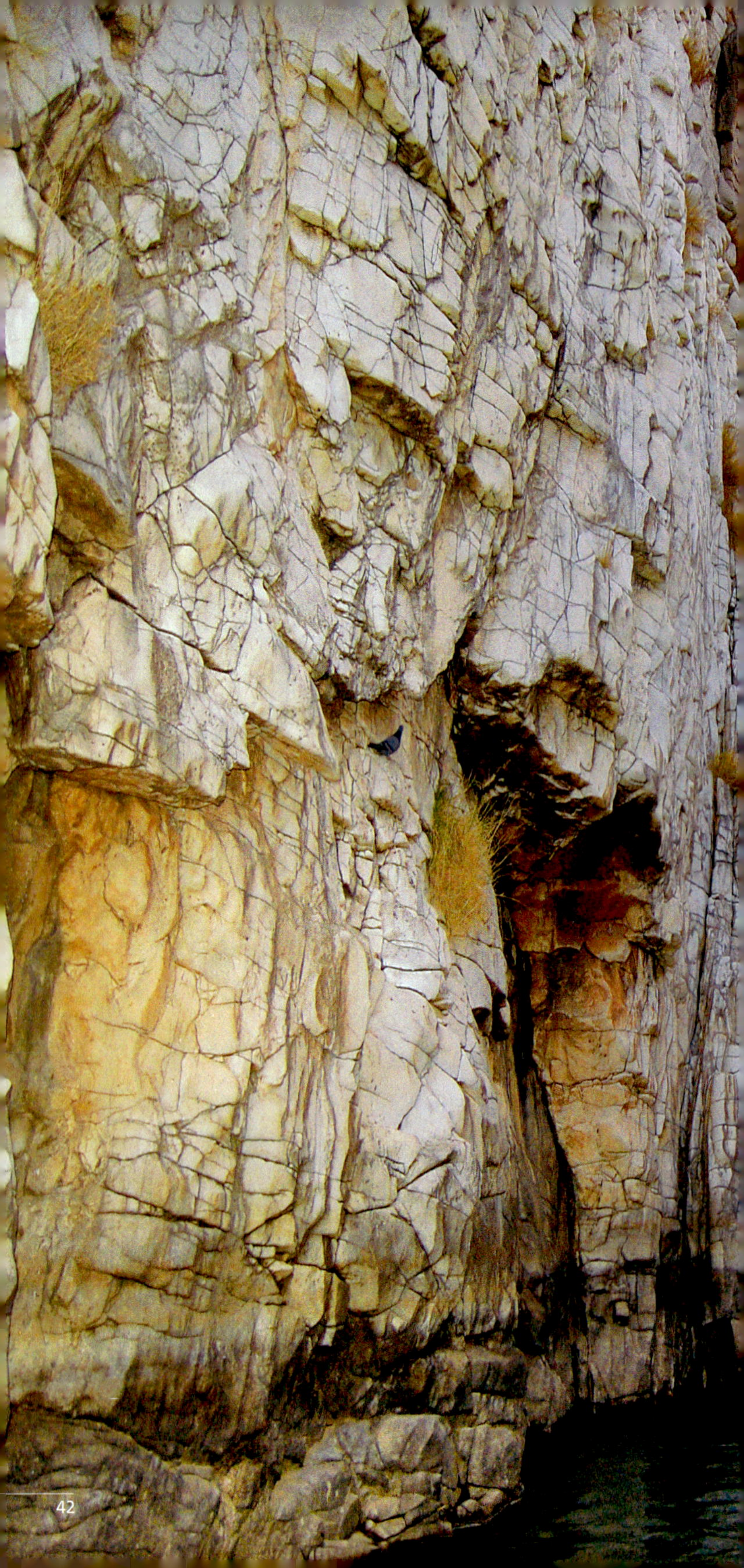

BHEDAGHAT

The small village of Bhedaghat is sacred as the confluence of Banganga with the Narmada. Some people equate the word *bheda* with *sangam* (confluence), and hence the name 'Bhedaghat'. The area has been, for centuries, a sacred ground for many rituals, which were mostly tantric in nature. Initially a tantrik *peeth*, it was known as Bhairava *ghati*. Tradition has it that it was here that the famous sage, Bhrigu, sacrificed himself to please Lord Shiva.

A much sought-after destination, Bhedaghat is visited by thousands of tourists every year, for its splendid Marble Rocks, Dhuandhar Waterfall and the 10th century Chausath Yogini Temple.

Marble Rocks

Soaring high in glittering splendour, the Marble Rocks at Bhedaghat rise to a hundred feet (30.5 m) on either side of the Narmada. Described by the *Imperial Gazetteer* as 'the tortuous gorge of white marble', the river here winds in a deep narrow stream flowing silently through high cliffs of magnesium limestone. Here and there the brilliant whiteness is tinted with veins of blue, pink and azure.

The tranquil beauty of the scene – the sunlight sparkling on the marble-white pinnacles and casting dappled shadows on the pellucid waters, has the ability to move even the most cynical mind.

Marble Rocks

One can best enjoy this 'miracle of nature' by taking a boat-ride to the Marble Rocks. The 30-minute ride takes one upto *bandar koodani* or the 'monkey-leap point', where the river runs through a very narrow gorge. 'Indra is said to have made this channel for the waters of the pent-up stream, and the footprints left on the rock by the elephant of the god still receive adoration.' A certain point in the river is famously called *bhool bhulaiya* – for though it appears to be a dead end, with cliffs closing the river on all three sides, on approaching closer one can find a passage on both the left and the right.

A moonlight boating trip on the river at this gorge presents a scene of almost unparalleled splendour.

> In his *Highlands of Central India*, Captain J. Forsyth writes: 'The eye never wearies of the...effect produced by the broken and reflected sunlight now glancing from a pinnacle of snow-white marble reared against the deep blue of the sky.'

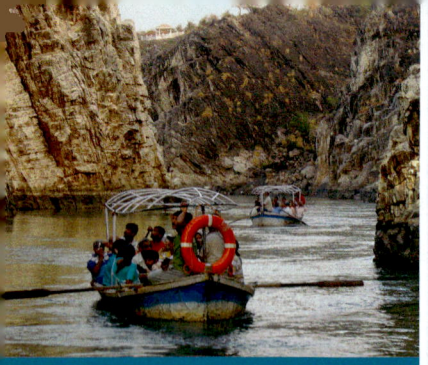

'With the entire stretch of water transformed into a sheet of liquid silver, the area is nothing less than a dream land!'

Boat charges:
Single person - Rs 30
Full boat - Rs 300
Due to the flooding of the river during monsoon, there is no boating from 15 June - 15 November.

Soapstone and French chalk are found in pockets in the bed of the Narmada and provide occupation to the many families of carvers in the region. Rows of stalls/ shops selling carved objects flank the steps leading down to the *ghat*. Images of deities (particularly Ganesha and Krishna), Shiva *lingas*, Nandi and crosses are crafted, along with candle/ *agarbatti* stands, and various exquisite decorative items. Walking along the *ghat*, one can watch the carvers at work, busy with their tools. Onyx, imported from Pakistan, is also being used now.

Marble Rocks

Though a day-trip can easily be made to Bhedaghat from Jabalpur city, it is perhaps not a bad idea to spend a night there to be able to fully enjoy the splendour of the Marble Rocks and the Falls. MP Tourism-run, Motel Marble Rocks is an ideal place for an overnight stay.

Located 6 kms from Bhedaghat, is the **Lamheta Ghat**, dotted with small shrines. It is also known as Paramhans Ghat as the Paramhans ashram stands right on its banks.

JABALPUR

Dhuandhar Falls

Further upstream is the Dhuandhar waterfall; Dhuandhar meaning smoke cascade. Here the Narmada leaves its wide bed and falls from a height of 30 ft (9 m) in a spectacular cascade. So powerful is the plunge that water droplets rise in a concentrated mass, creating an illusion of vapours or smoke, thus giving the falls the name 'Dhuandhar'.

Dhuandhar Falls

Even in winters, when monsoons have long been left behind, the volume of water is such that it gushes down at wondrous speed with a great roar! The three vantage points built right on top of the falls make for the best possible viewing. Standing by the falls, looking at the water gushing down and hearing its roar, the feeling is quite unlike any other.

The falls can be approached by car, or by walking down from the closest bridge. A ropeway to the falls has also been started recently, which gives a splendid view from the top.

JABALPUR

Chausath Yogini Temple

Built on a hillock, the Chausath Yogini Temple is approached by a long flight of steps, made out of the debris of the old monuments that stood here prior to the construction of the Yogini Temple.

Built by the Kalachuri king, Yuvarajadeva I in the 10th century, the temple is a hypaethral (wholly or partially open to the sky), circular structure with eighty-one peripheral chapels enshrining images of the sixty-four *yoginis* and other deities.

It is 'surrounded by a high circular wall… against the inside of which is built a veranda supported by columns set at regular intervals'. The largest *yogini* temple in India, it has a diameter of 41 m on the outside.

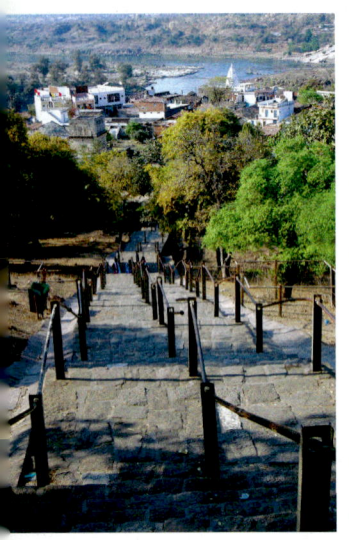

Above: *View from the top of the temple, with the stone steps leading down, and the Saraswati ghat visible in the distance*
Below: *The Chausath Yogini Temple*

Chausath Yogini Temple

Owing to its circular structure, it is refered to as Golakimatha. The temple structure is associated with the Shaivite tantric cult. Tantric rites like Chakra *puja* are believed to have been performed here.

Standing in the middle of the enclosure is the Gauri-Shankar temple, a relatively modern structure, said to have been built by the Kalachuri queen, Alhanadevi.

The temple has a *nagara*-style *shikhara*, and is built on a raised platform, with Shiva *lingas* in various sizes outside the entrance to the *garbhagriha*. The principal image in the *garbhagriha* is that of Shiva-Parvati riding astride Nandi, the bull. Lord Shiva is shown holding a *trishul* in his left hand, and Parvati, in her elaborate dress and ornaments, is shown holding a round mirror.

Above: *Circular cloister around the temple*
Below: *Shiva lingas just outside the main temple*

Above: *Sylvan surroundings of the ancient Chausath Yogini Temple*
Below: *Yogini, Sri Satnusamvara*
Facing Page: *Yogini, Sri Phanendri*

In Hindu mythology, the sixty-four *yoginis* are demi-goddesses who guide Sadhaks in the advanced stages of spiritual praxis. Although the origins of their cult are obscure, it arguably began around the 8th century due to the widespread dissemination of Tantra, with its radical inversion of gender constructs and militant deification of womankind.

The *yogi*, Matsyendranath (9th-10th century) is believed to have initiated the organisation of this diffused cult into a distinct sect of Tantrism, called Yogini Kaul Sampradaya, with an invocation of all 64 Yoginis at once, at the same spot in Bhedaghat on which now stands the Chausath Yogini Temple.

The temple priest claims this to be the only image of Shiva and Parvati on the bull, found anywhere in the world. Idols of Ganesha, Kartikeya and Laxmi-Narayana on their respective *vahanas* (divine vehicles) are also placed in the *garbhagriha*.

The circular wall around the temple is divided into panels, with magnificently carved sculptures in the niches. Of these 81 figures, 64 are *yoginis*, dating back to 10th century, and the remaining are dancing figures in red sandstone; mostly *saptamatrikas*, which some scholars attribute to the post-Gupta period. These sculptures are fine examples of medieval architecture.

53

JABALPUR

Above: Yogini, *Sri Sarvvatomukhi*
Above right: Detail from a pedestal
Below: Yogini, *Sri Varahi*

A *yogini* is the consort or female counterpart of a *yogi*, or 'an attendant of Goddess Durga' (as mentioned on the board at the temple site). Life-like in dimension, the *yoginis* are in a seated position, and have tantric symbols inscribed on them. The *yoginis* at this temple are not depicted as slender or comely, like the ones in the temples of Hirapur in Orissa, but have large and voluptuous bodies.

Bereft of an upper garment, they are ornamented with multiple necklaces, garlands, and a variety of bracelets and earrings, as is characteristic of Kalachuri art. The pedestals have carved images of animals on them. Unfortunately, most of the *yogini* sculptures are in a mutilated state, this condition not being recent, as even the *Imperial Gazetteer*, written over a century ago, mentions it.

Standing between the Narmada and Saraswati rivers, the Chausath Yogini Temple commands a singularly beautiful view of the Narmada flowing through the jagged Marble Rocks. According to a local legend, this ancient temple is connected to Durgavati's palace through an underground passage.

The site is now under the protection of the ASI or Archealogical Survey of India.

54

EXCURSIONS FROM JABALPUR

Jabalpur is the gateway to the three major wildlife parks in central India, Bandhavgarh, Kanha and Pench. It also serves as an entry point to the tourist destinations of Pachmarhi and Amarkantak.

Lesser known, though nevertheless worth seeing, are the close-by destinations of Bargi Dam, Mandla Fort and the National Park of Fossils, which make for interesting day-trips from Jabalpur city.

Bargi Dam
National Park of Fossils
Mandla Fort
Pachmarhi
Amarkantak
Wildlife Parks
Bandhavgarh
Kanha
Pench

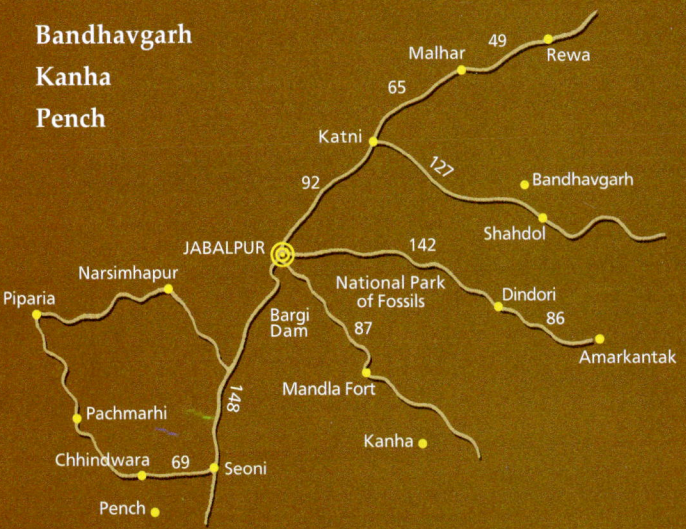

Sketch map not to scale

JABALPUR

BARGI DAM

Cruise Timings:
9 am - sunset
Charges:
Upper deck
Adult - Rs 75
Child - Rs 50
Lower deck
Adult - Rs 100
Child - Rs 50
Duration: 45 mins

Below: *Boating and cruise facilities available at the dam*
Facing page: *Views of the MP Tourism resort at Bargi Dam*

First ever multi-purpose project across the Narmada, the Bargi Dam is situated near Bijora village, around 40 kms southwest of Jabalpur city. It is a part of the Narmada Dam Project which aims at constructing 30 large hydroelectric dams on the river.

Completed in 1990, the dam stands 69 m tall and stretches to 5.4 kms in length. It is a major water source and is also used for power generation. The lake itself stretches to Mandla, which is 98 kms from Jabalpur.

The hour-and-a-half long drive to Bargi dam is through the small village of Bilhari, Gaur *nadi*, and Rani Durgavati's memorial, after which one enters an open landscape

Bargi Dam

with narrow, winding roads bound by hills, and scattered huts being the only sign of human habitation. Following a curve, the road suddenly looks out at a large body of deep blue water, seeming to appear out of nowhere. This is the Bargi Dam. The sight of the cobalt blue lake is breathtaking against the backdrop of green low-lying hills that surround it.

A popular tourist spot, its biggest attraction is a cruise on Bargi lake. The usual ride is for 45 minutes, however, there is also a six-hour cruise to Mandla, provided there are at least 15 passengers. One can also enjoy the waters on a paddle-boat or motor-boat. All activities are supervised by the MP Tourism-run Maikal Resorts at the site. It is well-equipped with a café with stunning views, and also offers accomodation.

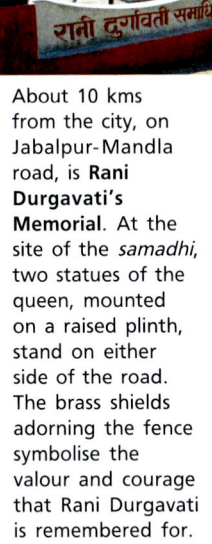

About 10 kms from the city, on Jabalpur-Mandla road, is **Rani Durgavati's Memorial**. At the site of the *samadhi*, two statues of the queen, mounted on a raised plinth, stand on either side of the road. The brass shields adorning the fence symbolise the valour and courage that Rani Durgavati is remembered for.

NATIONAL PARK OF FOSSILS

The best time to visit the park is from October to mid-February.

Situated in the Dindori district, the National Park of Fossils is 85 kms from Jabalpur. It was established in 1983 by the Madhya Pradesh Government for the display and preservation of the fossilised remains of many a prehistoric species found in various excavations in the state. Although covering a small area, the whole park is strewn with botanical fossils dating almost 40-150 million years ago, spread over seven villages of Mandla District (Ghuguwa, Umaria, Deorakhurd, Barbaspur, Chanti-hills, Chargaon and Deori Kohani).

MANDLA FORT

Mandla, 95 kms south of Jabalpur, is often visited for its fort. Built in the late 17th century, the fort stands in a loop of the Narmada in such a manner that the river protects it from three sides with a ditch on the fourth. Today the fort is subsiding into the jungle, though some of its towers still stand. Nearby on a stretch of the Narmada many temples dot the riverbank.

Pachmarhi

PACHMARHI

From Jabalpur, one can also go to Pachmarhi, the only hill station of Madhya Pradesh, situated at a distance of 240 kms. Tantalising the visitor with ancient cave paintings, clear, sparkling pools and the call of the wild in the dense woods of the Satpura ranges, Pachmarhi boasts of a number of 'tourist spots' within easy distance of each other.

MP Tourism today lists 28 must-see points. Bee Falls, now Jamuna Prapat, is Pachmarhi's primary source of water and offers a breathtaking sight. A visit to the Satpura National Park is a sure delight for all nature lovers.

The town derives its name from a group of five ancient dwellings hewn into the relatively soft sandstone of a low hill. Known as the Pandav caves, they are now protected monuments.

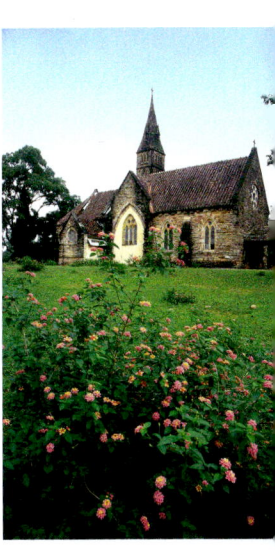

Above: *Catholic Church*
Left: *Verdant delights of Pachmarhi*

AMARKANTAK

Two great rivers of India, the Narmada and the Son, arise in the holy town of Amarkantak, in the north-eastern region of Madhya Pradesh, bordering Chhattisgarh. This small town of Amarkantak with its innumerable temples, holy ponds, and the surrounding forests is a sought-after destination both with nature-lovers as well as the spiritually-inclined.

An intricately carved Shiva-Parvati image on the wall of one of the old temples

Narmada Udgam, the temple built at the source of the Narmada is considered the holiest spot in the town. Every year on the occasion of Narmada Jayanti, the black basalt statue of the river goddess is covered with brocade and worshipped by fervent devotees.

Facing Narmada Udgam is the Mata Narmada Temple, a *shaktipeeth*. Adjacent to Narmada Udgam is an open pool called the Narmadakund. South of this *kund* are temples which were built by the Kalachuri king, Karnadeva (1042-1072).

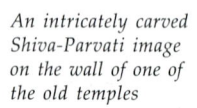

Around a kilometre from Narmadakund is Mai ki Bagiya, a grove of mango and banana trees, where goddess Narmada supposedly came to pluck fruits.

Six kilometres northwest of Narmadakund is the spectacular waterfall, Kapildhara. It provides a spectacular sight of a small stream turning into a mighty river, when it plunges 24 m down a cliff into a gorge.

Above: *Gushing waters of the Kapildhara*
Below: *The Narmada Udgam temple at Amarkantak*

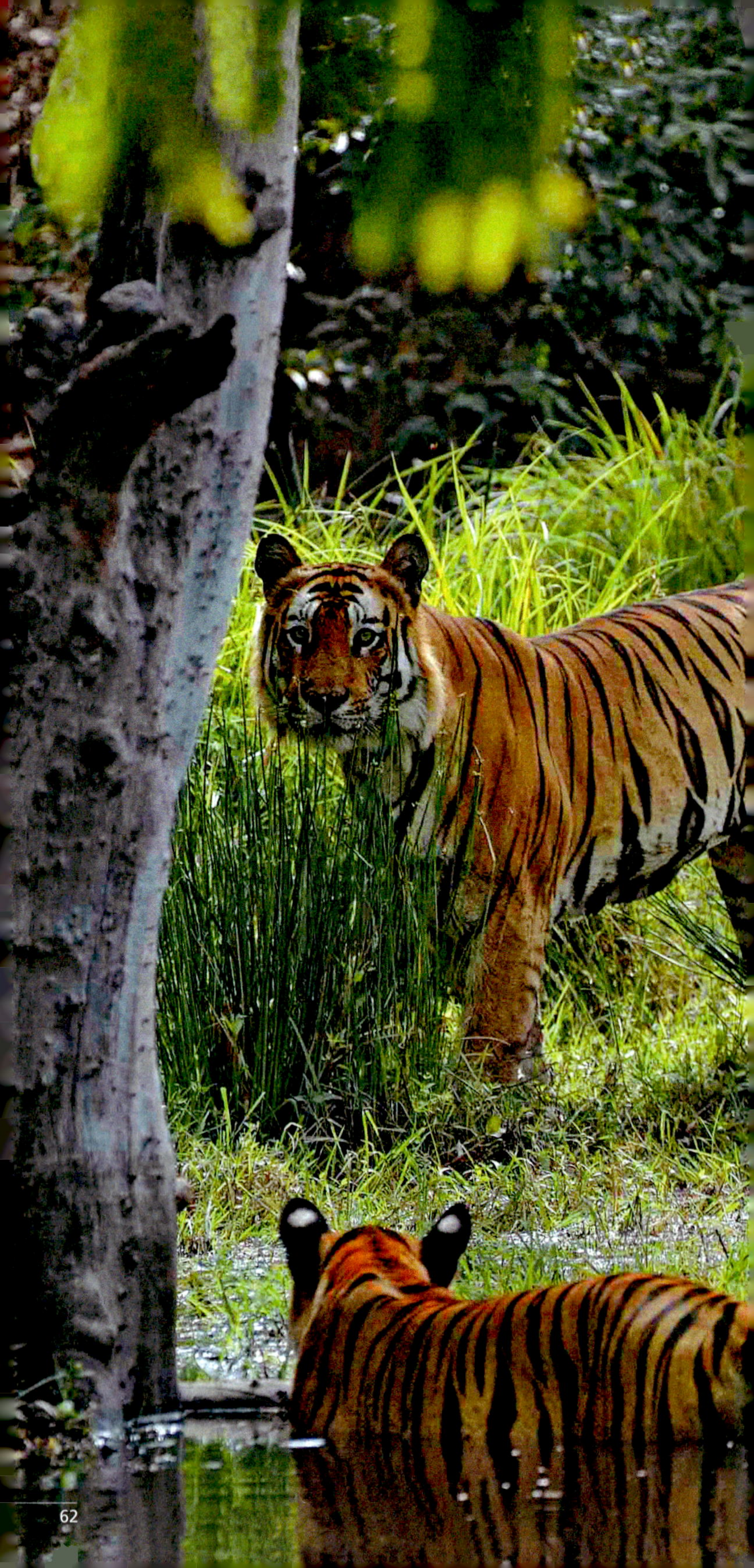

Wildlife Parks
Bandhavgarh, Kanha and Pench

The three major national parks of eastern Madhya Pradesh – Bandhavgarh, Kanha and Pench – are considered among the best in Asia, in general for the diversity of wildlife they support and particularly as habitats for India's national animal, the tiger. Bandhavgarh is a six-hour drive or 195 kms away from Jabalpur, while Kanha and Pench are, respectively, 175 and 200 kms away.

The three parks have a shared topography, since Bandhavgarh and Kanha are located on the eastern reaches of the Satpura range and Pench on its southern fringes. The terrain is primarily undulating, with mixed deciduous and sal forests interspersed with low-lying grasslands and occasional swampy marshes.

All three parks remain closed during the monsoons i.e., from 1 July - 30 September.

Bandhavgarh

There is more to Bandhavgarh than its enchanting natural beauty. There is a sense of antiquity, attributed to it by history and legend, that sets it apart from any other wildlife park.

According to the most famous of its legends, Rama, the hero of the epic Ramayana, stopped at Bandhavgarh as he returned home victorious from Lanka. Two monkeys, belonging to Hanuman's simian army, are said to have then built the Bandhavgarh Fort. Later, Rama handed it over to his brother Lakshmana, who assumed the title of *bandhavdhish* or 'Lord of the Fort', which is still used by the former Maharaja of Rewa.

Lakshmana is still worshipped in a temple within the Fort.

The sandstone caves to the north of the Fort have Brahmi inscriptions dating to the 1st century BC suggesting that there have been human settlements in the area for over 2,000 years.

From the early centuries of the 1st millenium onwards, Bandhavgarh was ruled by successive waves of rulers, including the Chandela kings of Bundelkhand. In the 12th century, it became the capital of the Baghels and remained thus till the early 17th century, when their descendants shifted their capital to Rewa. From then onwards, Bandhavgarh began functioning as a royal hunting preserve or *shikargarh* for the Maharajas of Rewa and their guests.

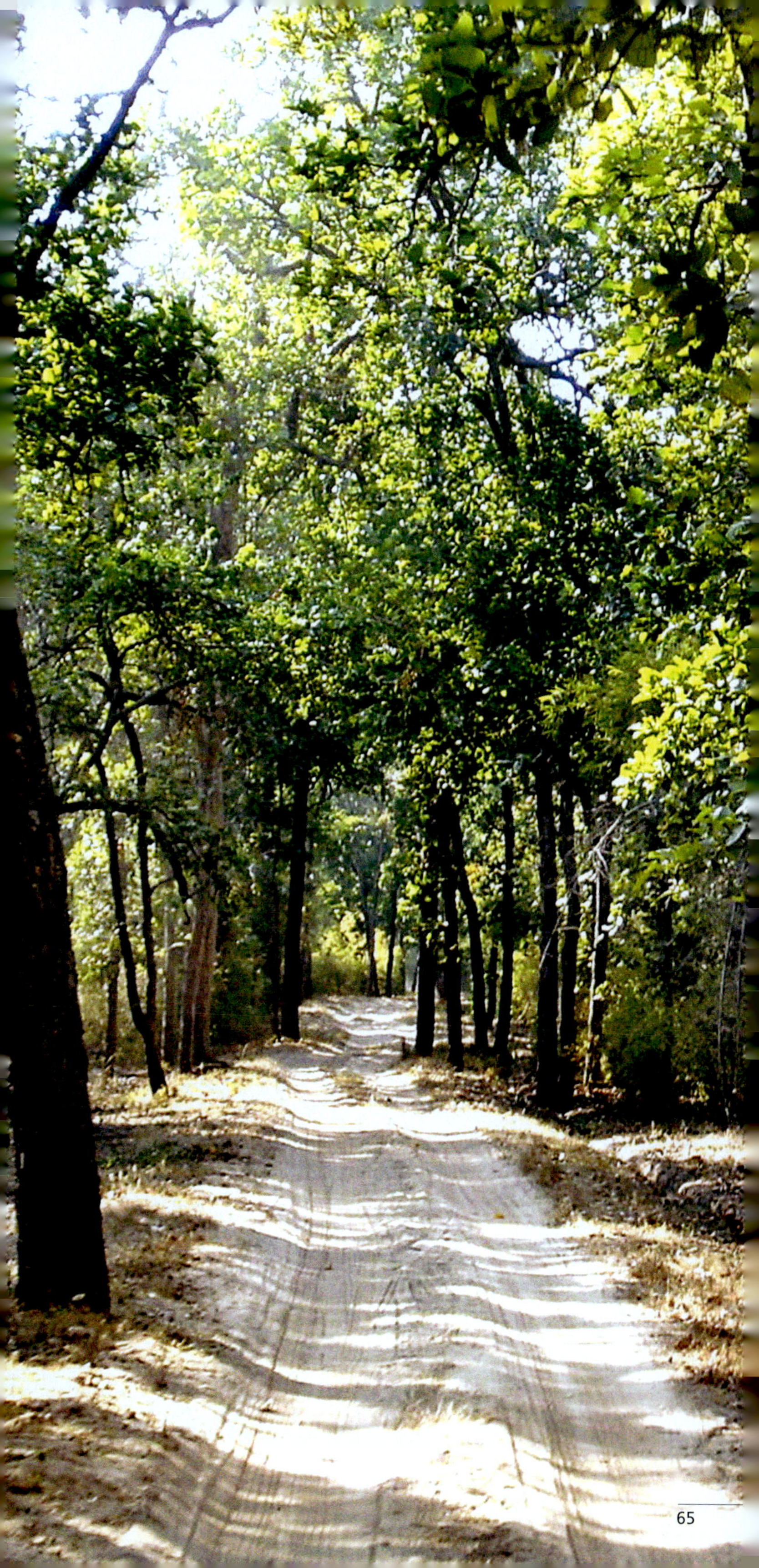

JABALPUR

Though the forests were spared from human encroachment, its tigers were ruthlessly hunted by the Maharajas, who felt compelled to uphold a cruel tradition of killing 109 tigers each. A particularly bloodthirsty royal, Gulab Singh of Rewa, boasted of killing 480 tigers in his lifetime!

After independence, with the abolition of the privy purses, the territories of the royals were taken over and Bandhavgarh became a part of Madhya Pradesh.

Above: *Langurs warn other animals of approaching predators from treetops*
Below: *The pride of Bandhavgarh, the majestic tiger*

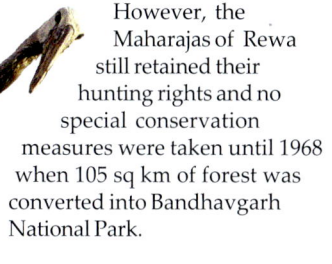

However, the Maharajas of Rewa still retained their hunting rights and no special conservation measures were taken until 1968 when 105 sq km of forest was converted into Bandhavgarh National Park.

Tigers were brought back from the brink of extinction, though their numbers increased substantially only after 1986, when the protected area was increased to 449 sq km. In 1993, Bandhavgarh was made a tiger reserve under Project Tiger.

Located in the Shahdol and Jabalpur districts of Madhya Pradesh, Bandhavgarh National Park is spread over an area of 1162 sq km. The original 105 sq km, known as Tala Range, serves as the principal viewing area. It comprises 32 rocky hills, with altitudes ranging from 200-1000 m, with the highest hill and the Bandhavgarh Fort atop it, at the centre.

Top: *Open-billed stork*
Above: *Chital stag*

Many streams run through the valleys, but only three are perennial. One of these, the Charanganga, has its source at the Fort, at a spot with an imposing 10th century statue of a reclining Vishnu called Sheshashaiyya. Through hundreds of years of wars and skirmishes, this water source has never been disturbed, because the Charanganga literally flowed from the feet of Vishnu.

There are four other ranges in the park, namely Magdhi, Kallwah, Khitauli and Panpatha.

Together the five ranges form the core area of the Park, spread over 625 sq km. Surrounding this is a buffer area of 537 sq km, which is spread over the forest divisions of Umaria and Katni.

Top: *Red-wattled lapwings cool themselves in a stream*
Above: *Sunset in Bandhavgarh*
Left: *Monolithic Vishnu as Sheshashaiyya at Bandhavgarh Fort*

JABALPUR

Kanha

Kanha National Park is located in the Maikal range, in the eastern sector of Satpura hills of the Central Indian Highlands. The name Kanha itself perhaps derives from the clayey soil at the bottom of the valleys in the region, locally called *kanhar*. Another legend attributes its name to a sage called Kanva who once lived in these parts.

Two river valleys are prominent in the Park's topography – the Banjar in the west and the Halon in the east. Both rivers are tributaries of the Narmada.

Shaped roughly like the figure '8', the park comprises a total area of 1,945 sq km. This consists of a core area of 940 sq km, surrounded by a buffer zone of 1,005 sq km.

For management purposes, the Park is divided into 5 ranges – Kisli, Kanha and Mukki in the western block, and Bhaisanghat and Supkhar in the eastern block. The latter two ranges are entirely closed to the public.

In the viewing area, one of the most beautiful areas of the Park from where a spectacular sunset can be seen is Bamni Dadar. The Park is served by an over-700 km network of fairly well-maintained roads.

Common Sandpiper

Although the first forest management rules for Kanha were instituted in 1862, it was not until 1933 that it was declared a sanctuary, though periodic shooting of deer and tigers was allowed. In 1955, however, concern about the depletion of tiger numbers led to the official designation of Kanha as a National Park. The main success of the Park's management in the years to come would be its rescue of the hardground barasingha (*Cervus duvauceli branderi*) from extinction. At the same time, it continued to play an important role in tiger conservation, and in 1973 was declared a tiger reserve, one of the original nine under Project Tiger.

During the 1980s, the popularity of the award-winning National Geographic film, *Land of The Tiger*, based mostly in Kanha, resulted in a dramatic increase in the annual number of visitors to the Park. The fact that the majority of visitors to Kanha are drawn by the prospect of seeing this magnificent animal in its natural habitat, makes tiger conservation inextricably linked with the future of the Park.

Above: *Purple Sunbird*
Below: *Nilgai*
Facing Page: *A sunlit jeep-trail in Kanha*

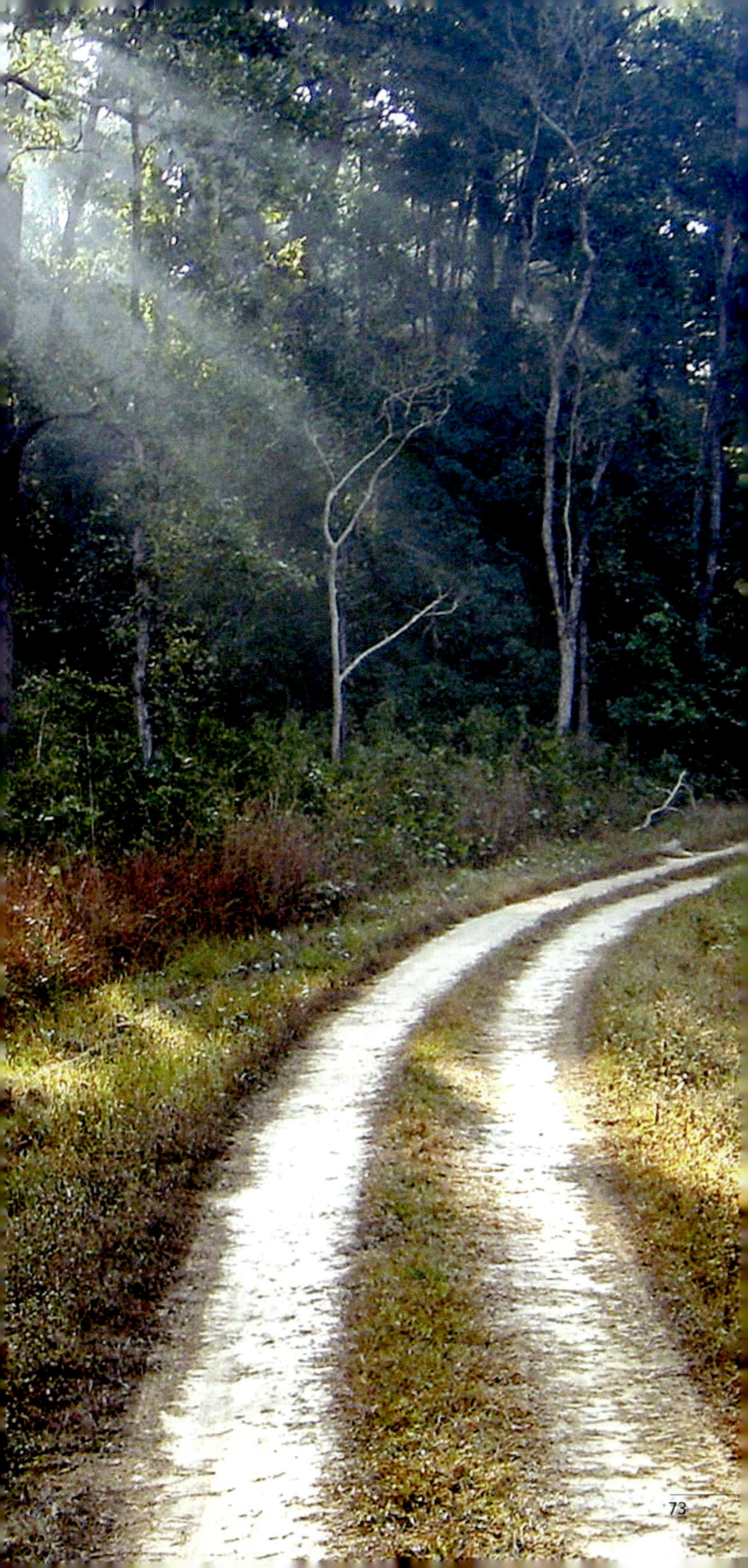

Pench

Pench National Park is situated in the once-thickly forested Satpura hills of Seoni and Chhindwara district. Before independence, the area had several game reserves used by the British. Post-independence, the need for ecological conservation became more urgent with much of the forest's large teak cover being depleted. In 1977, an area of 449.39 sq km was declared a sanctuary. In 1983, Pench National Park was carved out of the core zone of this sanctuary, spread over 293 sq km. Pench Tiger Reserve was created much later than the other reserves in Madhya Pradesh, in 1992, becoming the 19th reserve under Project Tiger.

75

JABALPUR

The National Park owes its name to the river Pench flowing through the centre of the Park, which divides it into the western Chhindwara Block (141.61sq km) and the eastern Seoni Block (145.24 sq km).

The Park has two entry points, at Ganda Tola and Kodajhiri, which have well-guarded forest barriers. The buffer zone of 465 sq km comprises 333 sq km of reserve forests, 102 sq km of protected forests, and 30 sq km of revenue land.

To provide a permanent water supply to the animals in the Park, many tanks have been dug. The main tanks are Chhindbari, Toyamit and Khamreeth. A few *nallahs*, such as Kharanda and Bamandoh, are used a storage tanks.

Above Left: *The commonly found* ber *fruit;* Right: *Sloth bear*

> Now these are the Laws of the Jungle
> And many and mighty are they
> But the head and the hoof of the Law
> And the haunch and the hump is – *Obey!*

The forests and grasslands of Pench and Kanha provided the magical setting of the Nobel Laureate Rudyard Kipling's famous *Jungle Book*, written in 1894. Kipling's story of the boy raised by wolves drew inspiration from William Henry Sleeman's pamphlet, 'An Account of Wolves Nurturing Children in Their Dens', which describes a wolf-boy captured in Seoni district near the village of Sant Baori in 1831.

Even today, when one visits Pench and Kanha, popularly referred to as Kipling Country, one can feel the tale and its characters come alive and can sense Mowgli and Sher Khan watching from a distance, away from prying human eyes.

Wildlife

Seasonal visibility of wild animals

The best time to visit the parks of eastern Madhya Pradesh is during the winter months (November to early March) that are cool, dry and delightful. The day temperature rarely goes above a comfortable 30°C, while the night temperature can dip as low as 2°C, with occasional frost. Since the monsoon has recently receded, the foliage is still green, though in the meadows, the severe frost can cause the grass to turn yellow. By mid-January, most deciduous trees begin to shed their leaves, only to be covered in bright green new growth by February. The large scarlet flowers which appear on the Semal trees are especially magnificent to behold.

The rutting season of many species of Indian deer occurs during the winter season. During December and January, one is likely to hear the haunting bugling calls of the hardground barasingha, unique to Kanha, echo across the meadows and even catch some spectacular stag-fights. Some species of deer, however, like the muntjac (barking deer) and chevrotain (mouse deer) are solitary and shy and offer mere fleeting glimpses at any time of the year.

One should also keep a lookout for the blackbuck, which is without doubt one of the most exquisitely built and coloured creatures in the wild. Post-independence, their numbers saw a steep decline, but thereafter, with a captive breeding programme in Kanha, rose again, though their present count cannot compare with that of the last century.

Above: *Wild boar*
Below: *Sambar*

JABALPUR

The summer months (March to mid-June) are hot and dry, with temperatures ranging from 42°C in the day to 20°C at night. Rains, if any, are sporadic, causing the grasses on the meadow to turn pale and parched. As the days get hotter, the rivers and *nallahs* begin to dry up. This water scarcity compels most animals, including the tiger, to concentrate near water areas.

Hence, during the steaming months of May and June, it is not unusual to spot tigers lying in secluded pools, or to see elephants and wild boar wallowing in water or mud. This is also the time when many mammals, predator and prey alike, visit salt licks to replenish their body stocks of vital minerals. A salt lick may be part of a hillside, a patch of earth or clay, or buried in the bed of a spring, lake, river or stream.

Among predators, the tiger, which is at the apex of the food chain, takes pride of place. Exuding majesty, grace and power, the tiger shows itself to a fortunate few in the wild, yet these forests and especially Kanha, are known as the best places in the world to spot them. Recent surveys, however, show alarming statistics of tigers remaining in the country's wildernesses, boding for a bleak future for India's national animal.

Leopards are the other big carnivores in these jungles, but they are rarely seen as the tiger population forces them to occupy low prey-density areas on the fringes of the forest.

Pre-monsoon showers in late June kill the heat and one can see massive deer congregations in meadows. This coincides with the second peak of the chital rutting season, the first peak being from mid-April to mid-May.

Wildlife

Foxes and jackals are often seen near herds of grazing chital, who remain unperturbed probably in the knowledge that these carnivores are in search of smaller prey. Chitals also share an interesting relationship with langurs. Langurs generally alert all in earshot with piercing calls at the approach of predators. Chital, and sometimes, wild boar follow the langur, also gobbling up pieces of fruit and leaves dropped on the ground in their untidy treetop foraging.

Soon after the monsoon breaks in mid to late June, the parks are closed to visitors. The foliage becomes resplendent and lush with new growth, but it also makes animals difficult to spot. The climate is humid and wet, with temperatures ranging from 20°C to 30°C. Also, as the rivers and *nallahs* are filled to bursting point, it encourages animals to disperse through the forest and makes sightings even harder.

National Park	Mammals
Bandhavgarh	Tiger, Leopard, Barking deer (Muntjac), Chausingha, Chinkara, Chital, Sambar, Rhesus Macaque, Wild Dog (Dhole)
Kanha	Tiger, Barasingha, Blackbuck, Sloth Bear, Gaur, Jungle Cat, Hyaena, Jackal, Dhole, Nilgai, Langur
Pench	Tiger, Chausingha, Chinkara, Chital, Sambar, Gaur, Sloth Bear, Dhole, Wild Boar

Spotting tigers in the wild is a matter of using one's senses to the maximum.

Tigers are masters of camouflage and this makes it easier for them to spot you without getting spotted themselves. One must therefore keep one's ears alert for warning calls by peacocks, sambar, spotted deer, langurs, jungle fowl and barking deer.

It also helps to train one's eyes on other animals such as the chital or spotted deer, which instinctively stand with their heads up and tails erect and repeatedly strike the ground with one of the forefeet when they sense a tiger or leopard nearby.

Another, and possibly the most significant, clue for tiger spotting, is the presence of vultures and crows on a tree or a cluster of trees, which frequently signals a kill by a predator on the ground.

Sometimes tigers give away their location by roaring, for instance, when calling out for a mate or when a chance encounter has led to a fight. But if it is just mildly disturbed, it only emits a low grumble.

Such sounds are, however, rare, and thus most park rangers and *mahouts* follow other indicators, such as tracks, droppings and most importantly, pugmarks, which are like the tiger's fingerprints.

Careful examination of these reveals all manner of information: sex, direction and rate of travel, presence of cubs with a mother, whether the animal has made a kill and so on. Some trackers can even tell the approximate time that tiger pugmarks were made.

Tiger Conservation

It is said that 40,000 tigers roamed the forests of India at the turn of the century. However, the first all-India tiger census conducted in 1972, revealed that there were only 1,827 tigers left in the wild. The need for a concerted effort to save one of the world's most magnificent beasts from extinction was already being voiced around the late 1960s, which had resulted in a national ban on tiger-hunting in 1970 followed by the passing of the Wildlife Protection Act in 1972.

In 1973, Project Tiger was launched as a 'Central Sector Scheme' with the full assistance of the Central Government and monetary support from the World Wildlife Fund. The Project aimed at conserving the vanishing home of the tiger by creating 'tiger reserves', in habitats as far removed from each other as Kanha in Madhya Pradesh, Sundarbans in Bengal, Corbett in UP and Periyar in Kerala. These reserves would be protected from human acts such as farming, felling of timber, overgrazing, fires, etc. while simultaneously involving local communities in management plans to create a symbiosis between forests, people and wildlife. The Project aimed at creating rich biotic zones outside the protected areas, to ensure the availability of fodder, fuelwood and wild foods to these communities. Minimising human intrusion in tiger habitat would not only reduce chances of human-tiger conflicts but also ensure prey for the tiger.

The immediate achievements of the Project were amply evident in the 1986 tiger census, which ascertained the increase of the tiger population in India to 4,005. Starting out with only nine reserves, there are 27 tiger reserves in the country today. As of 2006, Project Tiger has been incorporated into a body under the Ministry of Environment and Forests, Government of India, known as the National Tiger Conservation Authority, though the appellation 'Project Tiger' continues in popular usage.

A report published in January 2008 by the National Tiger Conservation Authority (NTCA) and Wildlife Institute of India (WII), Dehradun, places the current tiger population in the country at a worrying 1,411.

The report states that the tiger has lost much ground due to poaching to meet the increasing demand for the tiger's skin, bones (for traditional medicines) and pelts, as well as due to loss of quality habitat and loss of prey. Moreover, the jungle patrol is confessedly under-equipped — especially to take on poachers.

The findings of the report are that there are 89 tigers in Kanha whereas there were 127 in 2001-02*, 33 in Pench (as against 40 in 2000-01*) and 47 in Bandhavgarh (as against 56 in 2001-02*).

The NTCA believes that the current scenario requires a technology-oriented approach to curb wildlife crime. This would involve the creation of a widely distributed GIS-based Information Network, camera traps, radio-telemetry and DNA-based genetic studies to monitor tigers and their habitats.

It is worth mentioning that due to tireless campaigning by private tiger conservation bodies and individual conservationists, the Government of India is creating a hands-on vigilante task-force to counter poaching. But unless mankind is awakened to the devastating import of the extinction of the tiger, through education and active media support, they will not realise that it is, in fact, not only the tiger but the world itself, as we know it, which is at stake.

---

* http://projecttiger.nic.in/populationinstate.asp

The following are websites of government agencies and major organisations associated with tiger conservation, with special reference to Madhya Pradesh:

http://projecttiger.nic.in

http://projecttiger.nic.in/kanha.htm

http://projecttiger.nic.in/bandhavgarh.htm

http://projecttiger.nic.in/penchMP.htm

http://www.wwfindia.org

http://www.wii.gov.in

http://www.mpforest.org

Wild Etiquette

- Do not get down from your vehicle. Foot trekking is strictly prohibited.
- Do not feed the animals and keep a safe distance from them.
- Do not throw litter.
- Keep strictly to the road.
- Try to blend with the surroundings. Avoid wearing colours that jar.
- Do not make sudden or loud noises. Speak in hushed tones.
- Do not smoke inside the park. Negligence can lead to forest fires.
- Diesel vehicles are not allowed inside the park.
- Do not exceed the speed limit over 20 kms per hour.
- Refrain from using the car horn or headlights.

Birds of Bandhavgarh, Kanha and Pench

Racket-tailed Drongo (*Dicrurus paradiseus*) Considered the king of birds, this glossy black creature has two long streamers, each tipped with a racket. The forehead has a prominent tuft. Its fame is also partly due to its ability to mimic a host of other birds. Mostly visible in sal forests.

White-backed Vulture (*Gyps bengalensis*) Though its appearance is somewhat ungainly, it is also true, as Salim Ali observes, that there are few things as graceful as vultures riding the thermals high in the mid-morning sky. A conspicuous white band can be noticed on the under-surface of the wings as it flies.

Crested Serpent Eagle (*Spilornis cheela*) This handsome bird of prey is dark brown in colour and displays a prominent crest on the nape of the neck. The underparts have black and white bars. It favours wooded country.

Red-wattled Lapwing (*Vanellus indicus*) Little larger than a partridge, this handsome member of the plover family has a jet-black head, neck and breast and crimson-coloured wattles on its eyes. It is identified by a loud, familiar call that sounds like 'Did he do it?'.

White-eyed Buzzard (*Butastur teesa*) This bird of prey is about the size of a Jungle Crow, with a conspicuous white throat patch and yellowish-white eyes. Mostly seen in open, dry areas or where grass is being burnt.

Common Teal (*Anas Crecca*) Perhaps the commonest migratory duck in India, it is also one of the most attractive duck species in the region. The head of the male is chestnut brown with a broad green band extending from the eye to the nape of the neck.

White-necked Stork (*Ciconia episcopus*) This graceful bird, standing 85-100 cms tall, is mostly black, with the neck and the crown of the head white. Usually visible in the waterlogged areas of large meadows.

Indian Grey Hornbill (*Ocyceros birostris*) Measuring 60 cms, this grey-brown bird has a long tail tipped black and white and a large bill surmounted by a protuberance. An arboreal creature, it favours open country and can be tracked by its high-pitched squealing call.

Green Bee-eater (*Merops orientalis*) This richly coloured slender bird is no more than 16-18 cms in length, including the two elongated central tail feathers. It has green upper parts, though the colours of the head and underparts generally vary. Found in open country.

Red-wattled Lapwing

Wildlife

Flora

Arjun

Mahua

Kusum

Jamun

Amaltas	*Cassia fistula*
Aonla/Amla	*Phyllanthus emblica*
Arjun	*Terminalia arjuna*
Bamboo	*Dendrocalamus strictus*
Banyan	*Ficus bengalensis*
Ber	*Ziziphus mauritiana*
Bija	*Pterocarpus marsupium*
Dhawa/Dhaora	*Anogeissus latifolia*
Haldu	*Adina cardifolia*
Imli (Tamarind)	*Tamarindus indica*
Jamun	*Syzygium cuminii*
Kusum	*Schleichera oleosa*
Mahua	*Madhuca longifolia*
Mango	*Mangifera indica*
Palash	*Butea monosperma*
Saja	*Terminalia tomentosa*
Sal	*Shorea robusta*
Salai (Frankincense)	*Boswellia serrata*
Semal (Silk Cotton)	*Bombax ceiba*
Teak	*Tectona grandis*
Tendu	*Diospyros melanoxylon*

Sal

Imli pods

Bamboo

Imli

Teak

EDUCATION

Above: *Netaji Subhash Chandra Bose Medical College at Jabalpur is amongst the oldest medical colleges of Madhya Pradesh*
Below: *Mahatma Gandhi Institute of Nursing on the Jabalpur-Mandla road*

Jabalpur has an enviable set of educational establishments, which include more than 70 schools, three universities, and around 30 engineering and medical institutes. As a result, it serves the educational interests of not only its population of over a million but of the surrounding areas as well.

During the Gond period, Rani Durgavati's efforts made Jabalpur a centre of Sanskrit learning. Carrying along this tradition, Jabalpur was one of the earliest cities to impose compulsory education in 1928.

Owing to its strategic central location and a strong British presence during the colonial period, Jabalpur is home to a plethora of English-medium schools, many of them over a century old. The most important ones are – St. Xavier's, St. Aloysius, Christ Church (1876) and St. Joseph's Convent Girls School (1873). Besides, there are also the state-run Kendriya Vidyalayas (Central Schools), and numerous primary schools.

The two main universities in Jabalpur are the Rani Durgavati University and Jawaharlal Nehru Agriculture University (established 1950).

Robertson College is the oldest institution of higher learning in Madhya Pradesh. Named after the then Chief Commissioner, Sir Benjamin Robertson, it was previously known as Jubbulpore College. In 1955, it was renamed Mahakoshal Science College and was relocated in the Civil Lines. The illustrious alumni of the college includes the legendary Bollywood actor, Ashok Kumar.

A bill for the establishment of a university at Jabalpur was based on the recommendation of the Ramakrishna Commission, and was introduced in the legislature of the state in 1956. This University was later renamed Rani Durgavati Vishwavidyalaya in 1983. Its success can be gauged from the fact that today it is affiliated to more than a hundred colleges.

The Government Engineering College (1947), Medical College, Robertson College, Veterinary College (1948), and St. Aloysius College (1951), attract students from out of the city as well. Various polytechnics and vocational study-centres provide job-oriented courses to students. Jabalpur also has a number of research centres, for instance, the Tropical Forest Research Institute and the National Research Centre for Weed Science.

Its long tradition of learning has contributed to the growth of Jabalpur as a major centre of education. It is perhaps because of this that Acharya Vinoba Bhave called Jabalpur 'Sanskardhani' or the cultural capital of Madhya Pradesh.

PHRASE BOOK

IN EMERGENCIES

help!	bachao!
stop	rukho
medicines	davai
Please call a doctor/ambulance	doctor/ambulance ko bulaiye
Where is the nearest hospital?	nazdeek hospital kahan hain?
I'm not feeling well	Meri tabiyat theek nahin hai
Where is...?	Kahan hai...?
When will...be back?	...vaapas kabayenge?
Call the police	Police ko bulaiye

USEFUL PHRASES

How are you?	Aap kaise hain?
Very well, thank you	Hum theek hain, dhanyavad
What is your name?	Aap ka naam kya hain?
My name is...	Mera naam...hai
See you	Phir milenge
What is the time?	Kitna baja hai?
Where are you from?	Aap kahan se aaye hain?
Do you speak English?	Kya aap angreji bolte hain?
I don't understand	Maine nahin samjha
Please speak slow	Aap dheere-dheere boliye

SHOPPING

What is this?	Yeh kya hai?
clothes	kapda
shoes	joota
big	bara
small	chhota
black	kala
white	safed
red	lal
blue	neela
yellow	peela
green	hara
Do you have change?	Khule paise milenge?
Do you have...	Aap ke paas...hain?
How much does this cost?	Yeh kitne ka hai?
Do you take credit cards?	Aap credit card lete hain?
I'm just looking	Main sirf dekh raha hoon

USEFUL WORDS

hot	garam
cold	thanda
good	achcha
bad	bura
open	khula
close	band
left	baayen
right	daayen
near	paas
far	door
up	oopar
down	neeche
outside	bahar
inside	andar
fast	jaldi
slow	dheere
car	gaadi
bus	bus
road	sarak
way	raasta
house	ghar/makaan
door	darwaaza
fan	pankha
electricity	bijlee
train	train, railgadi
aeroplane	hawai jahaj

COMMUNICATION ESSENTIALS

greetings	namaste/namaskar
yes	haan
no	nahin
thank you	dhanyavaad/shukriya
money	paisa/rupaye
time	samay
day	din
night	raat
morning	subah
evening	shaam
afternoon	dopeher
today	aaj
tomorrow	kal
yesterday	kal
here	idhar/yahan
there	udhar/wahan
food	khana
water	paani
girl	ladki
boy	ladka
woman	aurat
man	aadmi
who	kaun
why	kyon
what	kya
where	kahan
when	kab
how	kaise
one/two	ek/do

PRACTICAL INFORMATION

WHEN TO COME TO INDIA

The best time to visit Jabalpur is between October and March when the average temperature is comfortable, varying between 8°C (46°F) and 29°C (84°F). The summer months of April to June are hot, with the maximum temperature rising upto 47°C (113°F). After the scorching heat, monsoons arrive towards the middle of June and stretch on till October. The level of the Narmada River rises greatly during monsoons, submerging the low-lying *ghats* around. During the winter months of December and January, day temperatures hover around a pleasant 12°C (54°F)' though nights can be very cold with the mercury dropping down to 2-3°C (36-37°F).

WHAT TO WEAR

India does not have a fixed dress code. *Sari* is the main attire for Indian women, but the easy-to-wear *salwar kameez* with *dupatta* is a popular option. *Kurta* and *pyjama*, along with sandals or leather *chappals* is a typical attire worn by Indian men. However, men wearing shirt and trousers, and women in western clothes are a common sight in big cities.

For the foreign traveller the general thumb rule would be to wear sensible, comfortable clothes that do not attract unnecessary attention. In case you are travelling during the hot Indian summer, loose cotton clothes that will protect you from the heat and keep you cool are ideal. It is advisable to wear a scarf or a hat to protect one's head from the blazing heat of the summer sun. Winter nights in Jabalpur can be quite freezing, so keep enough warm clothes if traveling during the months of December to February.

BEFORE COMING TO INDIA

There are a few things you need to take care of before travelling to India:

PASSPORT

Foreign travellers to India must always have a passport with them. You should ensure its validity for the entire period of stay. If your passport is lost or stolen, you should immediately contact the embassy or consulate of your country.

VISA

The tourist visa is normally given for six months. The 15-day single/double entry visa is issued only to bonafide transit passengers. Tourist groups of not less than four people, travelling under the auspices of a recognised travel agency, may be considered for a collective tourist visa.

A visa is given for a period for which the passport is valid. So, if the validity of the passport runs out before the visa expires, the visa is not issued. The visa is valid for 180 days from the date of its issue and not from the date of entry into India, unless specified otherwise.

TIME ZONE

Indian Standard Time (IST) is 5 ½ hours ahead of Greenwich Mean Time and 10 ½ hours ahead of US Eastern Standard Time. IST is 4 ½ hours behind Australian Eastern Standard Time, 3 ½ hours behind Japanese Standard Time and 1 ½ hours behind Thai Standard Time. Despite its vast geographical territory, India has just one time zone and no daylight saving time in summer.

STD CODES

New Delhi	011
Mumbai	022
Kolkata	033
Chennai	044
Bangalore	080
Hyderabad	040
Bhopal	0755
Indore	0731
Gwalior	0751
Jabalpur	0761
Pachmarhi	07578
Mandla	07642
Rewa	07662

PRACTICAL INFORMATION

VISA EXTENSION

The 180-day tourist visa is supposedly non-extendable but can be extended for another 15 days in case of emergencies. A valid onward ticket must, however, be produced as proof of the intention to depart the Indian shores. The 15-day extension on the 6-month visa can be issued by the Ministry of Home Affairs, New Delhi, the local State Government and the Foreigners' Regional Registration Office (FRRO). The FRRO office is open on weekdays, 9.30 am to 1.30 pm and 2 pm to 4 pm.

HOW TO GET THERE

BY AIR

Jabalpur airport – Dumna Air Strip – situated 18 kms from the city. It is linked by regular flights to Delhi and Indore.

BY TRAIN

Jabalpur railhead is situated on the main Mumbai-Howrah line and most trains on this route have a stop here. It is linked by direct trains from Delhi (Mahakoshal Express and Gondwana Express), Kolkata (Shakti Punj Express and Howrah-Mumbai Mail), Lucknow (Chitrakoot Express), Rajkot (Rajkot Express), and Bhopal (Jan-Shatabdi). Other major towns directly connected to Jabalpur are Mumbai, Varanasi, Allahabad, Durg, Madras, Hyderabad, Bangalore, Patna and Pune.

BY ROAD

The longest highway of the country, National Highway (NH) 7, connecting Varanasi to Kanyakumari, passes right through Jabalpur. It is connected both to neighbouring cities in the state, such as Nagpur, Raipur, Bhopal, as well as to other states by road. Transport buses to and from almost all cities of Madhya Pradesh frequent to Jabalpur. These can be taken from the main Bus Stand located near Corporation Chowk. Some private transport operators also have their luxury and semi-luxury coaches plying in and out of the city.

FRRO OFFICES

NEW DELHI
East Block 8, Level - II
Sector-1, RK Puram
Ph (011) 26711443/
384/ 074

MUMBAI
Annexe - II
Crawford Market
(near Police
Commissioner's Office)
Ph (022) 22621169/
0046

BHOPAL
Collector's Office
102 Old Secretariat
Ph (0755) 2538857

Registration for foreigners in Jabalpur can be done at the Police Commissioner's office at Malgodam Chowk.

Jabalpur airport inquiry
Ph (0761) 2901781

For timings and current status of flights log on to:
www.airindia.com
www.airdeccan.net
www.flykingfisher.com

For latest information on train schedules log on to:
www.indianrail.gov.in

For internet bookings:
www.irctc.com

DISTANCES FROM JABALPUR
(in kms)

Delhi	814
Mumbai	1125
Bhopal	261
Gwalior	487
Indore	494
Kanha	175
Bandhavgarh	195
Pench	200
Pachmarhi	240
Amarkantak	228
Rewa	204

PRACTICAL INFORMATION

MADHYA PRADESH STATE TOURISM DEVELOPMENT CORPORATION LTD (MPSTDC)

HEAD OFFICE
Paryatan Bhawan
Bhadbhada Road
Bhopal - 462 003
Ph (0755) 2778383/
     2774340/ 42-44
Fax (0755) 2779476/
     2774289
info@mptourism.com

MARKETING OFFICES

AHMEDABAD
219, 'Supermal' II Floor
Near Lal Bunglow, CG Road
Ahmedabad - 380 006
Ph (079) 26462977,
     32939000
Fax (079) 26462978
ahmedabad@mptourism.com

HYDERABAD
Counter No.6, First Floor
Balyoqi Paryatak Bhavan
Opp ITC Kakatiya Hotel
Begumpet Main Road
Hyderabad - 500 016
Ph (040) 32939000,
     40034319
Fax (040) 23407785
hyderabad@mptourism.com

KOLKATA
'Chitrakoot', Room No.7
6th Flr, 230 A
AJC Bose Road
Kolkata - 700 020
Ph (033) 22833526,
     32979000
Fax (033) 22875855
kolkata@mptourism.com

MUMBAI
45, World Trade Centre
Cuffe Parade Colaba
Mumbai - 400 005
Ph (022) 22187603,
     32539000
Fax (022) 22160614
mumbai@mptourism.com

NEW DELHI
Room No 12, Hotel
Janpath, Ground Floor
82-84, Janpath
New Delhi - 110 001
Ph (011) 23366528,
     23341185-87
Fax (011) 23347264
delhi@mptourism.com

NAGPUR
407-A, 4th Floor, Lokmat
Bhawan Wardha Road
Nagpur - 440 012
Ph (0712) 2442378,
     3259000
Fax (0712) 2423374
nagpur@mptourism.com

REGIONAL / TOURIST OFFICES

BHOPAL
Palash Residency
Near 45 Bungalow
TT Nagar
Bhopal - 462 003
Ph (0755) 2766750,
     25530066/ 67
bhopal@mptourism.com

City Booking Office
Palash Residency, Bhopal
Ph (0755) 2550588
ctobhopal@mptourism.com

Tourist Office
Railway Station, Bhopal
Ph (0755) 2746827
tobhopal@mptourism.com

JABALPUR
Railway Station
Platform No 1, Jabalpur
Ph (0761) 2677690
Fax (0761) 2677590
jabalpur@mptourism.com

GWALIOR
Tansen Residency,
6th Gandhi Road
Ph (0751) 2340370
Fax (0751) 2340371
gwalior@mptourism.com

Tourist Office:
Railway Station, Gwalior
Ph (0751) 4040777
togwalior@mptourism.com

INDORE
Shop No 10 & 11
Jhabua Tower, Ground Floor
RNT Road, Indore
Ph (0731) 2528653
Fax (0731) 2520345
indore@mptourism.com

KHAJURAHO
Chandella Cultural Centre
Khajuraho
Ph (07686) 274051
Fax (07686) 272330
khajuraho@mptourism.com

PACHMARHI
Amaltas Complex
Near Tehsil, Pachmarhi
Ph (07578) 252100
Fax (07578) 252102
pachmarhi@mptourism.com

JHANSI
Railway Station, Jhansi
Ph (0517) 2442622
tojhansi@mptourism.com

SATNA
Tourist Office
Railway Station, Satna
Ph (07672) 225471
tosatna@mptourism.com

UJJAIN
Tourist Office
Railway Station, Ujjain
Ph (0734) 2561544
toujjain@mptourism.com

KANHA
Khatia
Ph (07649) 277242
khatia@mptourism.com

BANDHAVGARH
White Tiger Forest Lodge
Umaria Road
Ph (07627) 265366
Fax (07627) 265406

PRACTICAL INFORMATION

HEALTH

Your health during your travel in India depends on three things: precautions taken before arrival, day-to-day care, and efficiency in tackling emergencies. Take care of what you eat or drink. It is best to carry your own mineral water. Bottled mineral water, aerated drinks, hot tea and coffee are easily available and are a good substitute for water. Guard against sunstroke and dehydration especially if you are travelling during the summer months. It would be useful to keep a packet of Electrol or any oral rehydration salts along with you and at the first sign of any kind of fatigue or dehydration to take it frequently with water.

MONEY

INDIAN CURRENCY

The Indian currency is called the Rupee. It is available in denominations of 1000, 500, 100, 50, 20, 10, 5, 2, 1. One rupee equals 100 paise. The coins in common use are those of Rs 5, 2, 1 and 50 paise. The 25, 20 and 10 paise coins have become redundant in bigger cities, but they still have value in smaller towns and in rural India.

CREDIT CARDS

Credit cards have become increasingly popular in urban areas. All major international credit cards including Visa, Amex, Mastercard, Diners Club are used in India.

BANKS

Banks are open from 10 am to 2 pm, Monday to Friday, and 10 am to 12 pm on Saturdays; most of them remain closed on Sundays and national holidays. A spate of international banks has opened branches in big cities, which have longer working hours. Jabalpur is dotted with ATMs (automatic teller machines) set up by banks. However, when travelling to smaller towns it is advisable to carry necessary cash because you may not find ATMs.

COMMUNICATIONS

TELEPHONE

ISD (international calls), STD (domestic long distance calls), and local telephone (calls made to local numbers within the city) can be made from the remotest corners of India. Most of the booths, at least in the larger towns, remain open till midnight and some even have facilities for sending and receiving fax messages.

PRIVATE HOSPITALS

Triveni Nursing Home
Gole Bazaar
Ph 2312538

Jabalpur Hospital and Research Centre
Russel Chowk
Ph 2408660

National Hospital
Gole Bazaar
Ph 2412612

Marble City Hospital & Research Center
North Civil Lines
Ph 2628254, 4045456

SC Gupta Memorial Hospital
Katanga Tower
Ph 2407152

GOVT. HOSPITALS

Govt. Medical College
Garha
Ph 2422113/ 17/ 18

Victoria Hospital
Near Omti Chowk
Ph 2621650

Cantonment Hospital
Ph 2622458

MONEY CHANGERS

State Bank of India
(Main Branch)
Civil Lines
Ph 623616

Three-A Travels
Near Bhanvartal Park
Bus Stand
Ph 4004455

EMERGENCY NUMBERS

Police	100
Fire	101
Ambulance	102

PRACTICAL INFORMATION

PRE-PAID TELEPHONE CARDS

The state-run MTNL now also offers facilities for buying pre-paid STD/ISD cards, which the consumer can use to make long-distance calls from any ordinary phone.

GENERAL POST OFFICE

Near Hotel Kalchuri Residency
Civil Lines
Ph 2621030, 2623094

COURIER SERVICES

There are several courier services available and most of them have at least one 24-hour service counter. It is advisable to insist on a receipt for payments made. For parcels over 20 kgs, a freight agent is required.

MOBILE PHONES

All travellers to India, except those from USA, Korea, Japan can use their mobile sets here. Those coming from the aforementioned countries need to have GPRS-GSM enabled sets. You can use your cell-phone in most places by buying a pre-paid SIM card from the local network service provider, by showing an identity proof. The foreigners need to show their passport for verification.

E-MAIL

Internet cafes are a common sight in the city. Internet browsing is relatively cheap and costs around Rs 20-30 per hour.

POST OFFICES

The main post offices provide a wide range of facilities like telegraph, fax and a courier service, which operates under the brand name EMS-Speed Post. Most of the post offices are open from 10.30 am to 3 pm on weekdays. Speed Post normally reaches in a maximum of two days in case of inland places and four days in case of foreign destinations.

LOCAL TRAVEL

For travelling within the city you can engage a local taxi, easily available at all hotels and taxi stands. Taxis and auto-rickshaws are often not metered and it is best to fix the rate beforehand, and to bargain. Taxis can also be booked from the MPSTDC Travel Counter at Hotel Kalchuri Residency, or the MP Tourism office at the railway station.

Auto-rickshaws and cycle-rickshaws are a common sight in most parts of urban and rural India, and are a convenient means of covering short distances. However, for those on a budget it is best to travel by bus, both within the city and outside it. There are buses run by the local state governments as well as by private operators. The luxury buses charge higher fares and provide you with frills like air-conditioning and even reclining seats, however these operate only on inter-city routes. One thing is certain whatever the kind of bus you board, the ride can be both bumpy and crowded, but if you are the kind who likes to travel *impromptu* they are definitely the quickest way to reach your destination.

CAR RENTALS

There are several international and local companies that operate car rental services in major Indian cities. The rates of hiring a car depend on the choice of car and whether it is chauffeur driven. For self-driven cars, besides the rental charges the petrol cost is to be borne by the customer. A valid driving license, passport (for foreigners) or proof of address is required along with a security deposit.

PRACTICAL INFORMATION

TOURS & GUIDES
Tours within the city, as well as to Bhedaghat, wildlife parks of Bandhavgarh, Kanha and Pench, and to the hill-station of Pachmarhi can be organised by the MP Tourism Department, on ones desired dates and duration. However, the tours are organised for a group of minimum 4 people. If less than 4, the extra cost of the package will have to be borne.

WHERE TO STAY IN AND AROUND JABALPUR

JABALPUR

LUXURY

Narmada Jacksons
(A Welcom Heritage Hotel) South Civil Lines
Ph (0761) 4001122, 2677663
Fax (0761) 4011000
hoteljacksons@hotmail.com

Kalchuri Residency
(MPSTDC)
Civil Lines
Ph (0761) 2678491-92
Fax (0761) 2678493
kalchuri@mptourism.com

The Samdariya
789, Russel Chowk
Ph (0761) 4004132/ 34
Fax (0761) 2402354
samdariyahotel@sify.com

Hotel Satya Ashoka
Wright Town Stadium
Ph (0761) 2415111-13
Fax (0761) 4016858
hotelsatyaashoka@hotmail.com

Hotel Rishi Regency
Opposite State bank of India, Civil Lines
Ph (0761) 4046001-04, 2623623
Fax (0761) 2623904
jabalpur@hotelrishiregency.com

Hotel Gulzar Towers
Nagpur Highway
Ph (0761) 4070100, 4070300
Fax (0761) 4070300
gulzartowers@yahoo.co.in

MODERATE

Arihant Palace
958 Main Russel Crossing
Ph (0761) 2627311/ 12,
Fax (0761) 2692114
enquiry@arihantpalace.com

Hotel Roopali
859, Station Road
Napier town
Ph (0761) 4004040, 2625567/ 68
Fax (0761) 2625569
hotelroopali@mantrafreenet.com

Hotel Shikhar Palace
Russel Chowk
Ph (0761) 2629172/ 73,
Fax (0761) 2692114

Hotel Krishna
Bhanvartal Extension
Ph (0761) 4004023/ 24, 2403318
Fax (0761) 2412253
krishnahotel@hotmail.com

Hotel Prestige Princess
Nagrath Square
Ph (0761) 2627550-53
Fax (0761) 2627554
hprestigeprincess@rediffmail.com

BUDGET

Hotel Samrat
Russel Chowk
Ph (0761) 4004218

Hotel Rahul
Opposite Jyoti Cinema
Ph (0761) 2625525

Hotel Mayur
Malviya Chowk
Ph (0761) 4006374

BHEDAGHAT

Motel Marble Rocks
(MPSTDC)
Ph (0761) 2830424
Fax (0761) 2830346
mmr@mptourism.com

Shagun Resorts
Ph (0761) 3296061

Rocks Palaces
Ph (0761) 2830345

Hotel Adersh
Ph (0761) 3291264

BARGI DAM

Maikal Resorts (MPSTDC)
Ph (0761) 2904577
mrbargi@mptourism.com

PACHMARHI

Amaltas (MPSTDC)
Ph (07578) 252098
amaltas@mptourism.com

Club View (MPSTDC)
Ph (07578) 252801
cview@mptourism.com

Glen View (MPSTDC)
Ph (07578) 252533, 252445
gview@mptourism.com

Hilltop Bungalow
(MPSTDC)
Ph (07578) 252846
hilltop@mptousism.com

PRACTICAL INFORMATION

Panchvati Cottages
(MPSTDC)
Ph (07578) 252096
panchvati@mptourism.com

Rock-End Manor
(MPSTDC)
Ph (07578) 252079
rem@mptourism.com

Satpura Retreat (MPSTDC)
Mahdeo Road
Ph (07578) 252097
satpura@mptourism.com

KANHA

Baghgira Log Huts
(MPSTDC)
Kisli
Ph (07649) 277227/ 242
blh@mptourism.com

Kanha Safari Lodge
(MPSTDC) Mukki
Ph (07636) 290715
    (07637) 226029
ksl@mptourism.com

Tourist Hostel (MPSTDC)
Kisli
Ph (07649) 277310
thk@mptourism.com

Krishna Jungle Resort
Khatia village
Ph (07649) 277207/ 208
krishnahotel@hotmail.com

Royal Tiger Resort
Mukki village
Ph (07637) 216028

Tuli Tiger Resorts
Kisli village
Ph (07649) 277221,
    277251
sales@tuligroup.com

BANDHAVGARH

White Tiger Forest Lodge
(MPSTDC)
Ph (07627) 265366,
    265308
Fax (07627) 265308
wtfl@mptourism.com

Tiger Trail Resort
Ph (07627) 265325

Mahua Kothi
(Taj & CC Africa)
Village Tala, Umaria
Ph (07627) 265402/ 14
Fax (07627) 265400
mahua.kothi@tajhotels.com

Mogli Jungle Resort
Village Tala, Umaria
Ph 9425156245
resortmogli@yahoo.com

PENCH

Kiplings Court (MPSTDC)
Avarghani village
Ph (07695) 232830
kcpench@mptourism.com

Pench Jungle Camp
Avarghani village
Ph (07695) 232817
jaidevsingh_rathore@
yahoo.com

Bagh Van Lodge
(Taj Property)
Avarghani village, Seoni
Ph (07695) 232829
baghvan.pench@
tajhotels.com

WHERE TO EAT

Jabalpur has a variety of restaurants to choose from. The Indian Coffee House in Sadar Bazaar and Maikal restauraunt in MP Tourism-Kalchuri Residency are very popular. They offer a great variety and are value for money.

For those willing to spend, exploring the multi-cuisine restaurants in the various luxury hotels is an excellent option – Grub Room in Narmada Jacksons, Haveli in Hotel Krishna, Zayaka in Rishi Regency, and Daavat in Samdariya. Amrapali restaurant in Hotel Siddharth; Panchvati Gaurav (for Rajasthani cuisine) and Option at Marhatal; and Traffic Jam at Sadar Bazaar are among the more reasonable options.

WHERE TO SHOP

Sadar Bazaar is the main shopping centre in the Cantonment area. Perhaps the cleanest and the most upmarket of all bazaars, one can get everything here, from clothes, shoes, accessories to articles of daily use. There are several shops here where one can pick the traditional Maheshwari, Chanderi saris and Bagh prints. The Treasure Island Mall, which will have all brand outlets, is under construction.

If you are not averse to crowds and to bargaining, the bazaars in the old city make for a good experience. One can shop at the Gorukhpur Bazaar, Bada Phuvvara or Omti Nala.

PRACTICAL INFORMATION

BANDHAVGARH NATIONAL PARK

Jabalpur, the nearest airport (195 kms), is well connected to the Park by road and rail.

BY RAIL

To reach Bandhavgarh from Jabalpur take a train to Katni, the nearest railway station, from where you can drive down to Tala (75 kms). Alternatively board a train, from Jabalpur for Umaria on the Katni-Bilaspur section of South-Eastern Railways, and from there onwards, take a bus or a jeep to Tala (30 kms). In case you are coming from Khajuraho, Varanasi or Kolkata, the most convenient railhead would be Satna (117 kms).

BY ROAD

To go by road from Jabalpur to Bandhavgarh drive down to Shajpura (144 kms) then take a country road to Umaria. In case you are coming from Khajuraho (230 kms) you can take a taxi from Satna (5 hours) to Umaria.

LOCAL TRAVEL

Tala, a small village, is the main entry-point to the park. You can rent a jeep from the park office or any of the hotels located here. A package tour which includes a guide, entry fees and vehicle fees for a single trip into the park costs around Rs 1380 (2-3 hrs for 4-6 persons).

KANHA NATIONAL PARK

Jabalpur is 175 kms from Kanha (Kisli gate) via Mandla, the nearest large town.

BY AIR

Jabalpur is the nearest airport connected by regular flights to Delhi and Indore. Nagpur, in Maharashtra, is 226 kms away and is connected by regular flights to Delhi, Bhopal, Mumbai and Kolkata.

BY RAIL

The nearest railway station is also at Jabalpur, from where trains ply to all major metros and large cities of Madhya Pradesh.

BY ROAD

The main gates of Kanha National Park are at Kisli and Mukki villages separated by a distance of 33 kms. Daily buses depart from Jabalpur to Kisli via Mandla. A direct bus also leaves from the Jabalpur railway station for Kanha (6 hrs) in time for the park transport. In case you reach the park after dark you will have to stay at Kisli since entry into the park after sunset is prohibited.

Note that diesel vehicles are disallowed within all Parks.

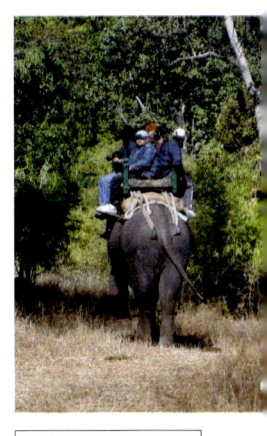

For information contact: Director Bandhavgarh National Park, P O Umaria District Shahdol - 484661
Ph (07563) 222214

Park Timings:
Sunrise to Sunset
Entry fee:
Rs. 2000 (foreigners)
Rs. 530 (Indians)
Elephant ride: Rs 150
Guide fee: Rs 150
Jeep (MPSTDC):
Rs 700 (for 6 persons, inclusive of two trips, between 0530-0930 and 1600-1900 hrs)

For further information contact: Conservator & Field Director
Kanha Tiger Reserve
Ph (07642) 250760
Fax (07642) 251266
cfkanhanpmal@mp.nic.in

95

PRACTICAL INFORMATION

LOCAL TRAVEL

Jeep tours organised by the Forest department start at Kisli (0600-1800) and you even have the option to share the jeep with others for economy. MPSTDC also operates a jeep service for visitors to go around in the park. Self-driven jeeps can be hired from the MPSTDC Office at Kisli, which also offers the services of guides on payment of a nominal amount. Wild Chalet Resorts at village Mocha can also arrange for local sightseeing tours. The park authorities organise elephant rides, which begin from Kisli, Kanha and Mukki. For bookings contact the Range Officer (Kanha, Kisli or Mukki) or the Manager, Baghira Log huts, Kisli and Kanha Safari Lodge, Mukki.

There are visitor centres at Khatia and Mukki gates and the largest is at Kanha. They have informative displays, short films, audio-visual shows and books for sale.

PENCH NATIONAL PARK

Pench is one of the most easily accessed national parks. It is 12 kms away from Khawasa on NH 7 between Nagpur and Jabalpur. Khawasa is 81 kms from Nagpur and 193 kms from Jabalpur. The main entrance to the park is from Turia and another less used entrance is at Karmajhiri.

For further information contact:
The Field Director
Pench National Park
Seoni
Telefax (07692) 223794

BY AIR

The nearest airport from Pench is at Jabalpur (appx. 200 kms).

BY TRAIN

The nearest railhead is at Seoni (30 kms), however none of the major trains halt here. Nagpur, two-hours from Pench by road is the best option from Delhi and Mumbai. Jabalpur which is around a 4-5 hours drive by road from Pench is the other largest railhead.

BY ROAD

Pench is situated on the Nagpur-Jabalpur highway and is easily accessible by local taxis. However, if you take a bus from Nagpur, get off at a small town called Khawasa, which is the turning point from the highway for Turia (13 kms). Suktara is the turning point for Karmajhiri (30 kms).

LOCAL TRAVEL

Visitors can explore the park in their own cars or jeeps along with a registered guide. Alternately the resort where you are staying can arrange for safari vehicles some of which are specially designed for wildlife sighting. Specially organised nature walks are conducted by wildlife department guides, from Raiyakassa to Karmajhiri. Elephant rides are available from Alikatta and are an ideal way to experience the jungle.

Photographs on p 69 Below: Ananda Banerjee; p 83: Mallar Sarkar